G000022344

NUCLEAR TERRORISM

RESPONSE PREPAREDNESS ISSUES OF MAJOR CITIES

TERRORISM, HOT SPOTS AND CONFLICT-RELATED ISSUES

Additional books in this series can be found on Nova's website under the Series tab.

Additional E-books in this series can be found on Nova's website under the E-book tab.

TERRORISM, HOT SPOTS AND CONFLICT-RELATED ISSUES

NUCLEAR TERRORISM

RESPONSE PREPAREDNESS ISSUES OF MAJOR CITIES

CASEY A. LLOYD
EDITOR

New York

For permission to use material from this book please contact us:
Telephone 631-231-7269; Fax 631-231-8175
Web Site: http://www.novapublishers.com

Library of Congress Cataloging-in-Publication Data

ISBN: 978-1-62948-696-3

Published by Nova Science Publishers, Inc. † New York

CONTENTS

PREFACE

A terrorist attack in a major city using an RDD or an IND could result not only in the loss of life but also have enormous psychological and economic impacts. Major cities are assumed to be preferred targets of such attacks, and local governments, along with their states, have primary responsibilities for early response (within the first 24 hours), with assistance from federal sources, as necessary, coming later. A disjointed or untimely response could increase the impact and undermine public confidence in federal, state and local governments' ability to respond to an attack. This book provides background for understanding the RDD threat and responses, and presents issues for Congress.

Chapter 1 - A terrorist attack in a major city using an RDD or an IND could result not only in the loss of life but also have enormous psychological and economic impacts. Major cities are assumed to be preferred targets of such attacks, and local governments, along with their states, have primary responsibilities for early response (within the first 24 hours), with assistance from federal sources, as necessary, coming later. A disjointed or untimely response could increase the impact and undermine public confidence in federal, state and local governments' ability to respond to an attack.

GAO was asked to review issues related to response preparedness for RDD and IND attacks. This report examines major cities' (1) assessment of RDD and IND risks and development of response plans, (2) perceptions of their abilities to respond within the first 24 hours, and (3) perceptions of the need for federal support in early response to these attacks. GAO primarily relied on questionnaire responses from emergency managers of 27 of the 31 major cities that the Department of Homeland Security considers to be at high risk for terrorist attack, the review of pertinent federal guidance, and interviews with FEMA officials and others.

Chapter 2 - Congress has long sought, through legislation and oversight, to protect the United States against terrorist threats, especially from chemical, biological, radiological, and nuclear (CBRN) weapons. Radiological dispersal devices (RDDs) are one type of CBRN weapon. Explosive-driven "dirty bombs" are an often-discussed type of RDD, though radioactive material can also be dispersed in other ways. This report provides background for understanding the RDD threat and responses, and presents issues for Congress.

Radioactive material is the necessary ingredient for an RDD. This material is composed of atoms that decay, emitting radiation. Some types and amounts of radiation are harmful to human health.

Terrorists have shown some interest in RDDs. They could use these weapons in an attempt to cause panic, area denial, and economic dislocation. While RDDs would be far less harmful than nuclear weapons, they are much simpler to build and the needed materials are used worldwide. Accordingly, some believe terrorists would be more likely to use RDDs than nuclear weapons. Key points include:

- RDDs could contaminate areas with radioactive material, increasing long-term cancer risks, but would probably kill few people promptly. Nuclear weapons could destroy much of a city, kill tens of thousands of people, and contaminate much larger areas with fallout.
- Cleanup cost after an RDD attack could range from less than a billion dollars to tens of billions of dollars, depending on area contaminated, decontamination technologies used, and level of cleanup required.
- Terrorists would face obstacles to using RDDs, such as obtaining materials, designing an effective weapon, and avoiding detection.

Governments and organizations have taken steps to prevent an RDD attack. Domestically, the Nuclear Regulatory Commission has issued regulations to secure radioactive sources. The Department of Homeland Security develops and operates equipment to detect radioactive material. The National Nuclear Security Administration has recovered thousands of disused or abandoned sources. Some state and local governments have taken steps to prepare for an RDD attack. Internationally, the International Atomic Energy Agency has led efforts to secure radioactive sources. Its Code of Conduct on the Safety and Security of Radioactive Sources offers guidance for protecting sources. The G8 Global Partnership has secured sources in Russia and elsewhere. Other nations have taken steps to secure sources as well. Key points include:

- Nuclear Regulatory Commission actions have done much to instill a security culture for U.S. licensees of radioactive sources post-9/11.
- Many programs have sought to improve the security of radioactive sources overseas, but some incidents raise questions about security.

Should prevention fail, federal, state, and local governments have taken many measures to respond to and recover from an RDD attack. The National Response Framework "establishes a comprehensive, national, all-hazards approach to domestic incident response." The federal government has expertise and equipment to use for recovery. Key points include:

- Government agencies have done much to prepare for and recover from an RDD attack. This work would help cope with other disasters. Conversely, planning for other disasters would help in the event of an RDD attack.
- Response planning fell short in the wake of Katrina and the Gulf oil spill, raising questions about the effectiveness of planning to respond to an RDD attack.

Issues for Congress include:

- The priority for countering RDDs vs. other types of CBRN weapons.
- The proper balance of effort for securing domestic vs. overseas radioactive sources.
- Whether to establish a radiation detection system in cities; how to dispose of potentially large volumes of radioactive waste that could result from an RDD attack.
- Whether to modify the pace of a program for implementing certain security enhancements for U.S. radioactive sources.
- How to improve radiological forensics capability.

In: Nuclear Terrorism   ISBN: 978-1-62948-696-3
Editor: Casey A. Lloyd   © 2014 Nova Science Publishers, Inc.

Chapter 1

NUCLEAR TERRORISM RESPONSE PLANS: MAJOR CITIES COULD BENEFIT FROM FEDERAL GUIDANCE ON RESPONDING TO NUCLEAR AND RADIOLOGICAL ATTACKS[*]

United States Government Accountability Office

WHY GAO DID THIS STUDY

A terrorist attack in a major city using an RDD or an IND could result not only in the loss of life but also have enormous psychological and economic impacts. Major cities are assumed to be preferred targets of such attacks, and local governments, along with their states, have primary responsibilities for early response (within the first 24 hours), with assistance from federal sources, as necessary, coming later. A disjointed or untimely response could increase the impact and undermine public confidence in federal, state and local governments' ability to respond to an attack.

GAO was asked to review issues related to response preparedness for RDD and IND attacks. This report examines major cities' (1) assessment of RDD and IND risks and development of response plans, (2) perceptions of their abilities to respond within the first 24 hours, and (3) perceptions of the

[*] This is an edited, reformatted and augmented version of a Highlights of GAO-13-736, a report to the Chairman, Committee on Homeland Security and Governmental Affairs, U.S. Senate, dated September, 2013.

need for federal support in early response to these attacks. GAO primarily relied on questionnaire responses from emergency managers of 27 of the 31 major cities that the Department of Homeland Security considers to be at high risk for terrorist attack, the review of pertinent federal guidance, and interviews with FEMA officials and others.

WHAT GAO RECOMMENDS

GAO recommends that FEMA develop guidance to clarify the early response capabilities needed by cities for RDD and IND attacks. FEMA did not concur with this recommendation. GAO believes that gaps in early response abilities warrant federal attention and has clarified its recommendation.

WHAT GAO FOUND

Many emergency managers from the 27 major cities responding to GAO's questionnaire, although not all, reported that their city had assessed the risks of a terrorist attack using a radiological dispersal device (RDD) or improvised nuclear device (IND) and had ranked the risk of these attacks as lower than the risk of other hazards they face. Also, 11 of the 27 reported that they had completed RDD response plans, and 8 of the 27 reported that they had completed IND response plans. Some emergency managers for cities without specific RDD and IND response plans reported that they would rely on their city's all hazards emergency operations plan or hazard management plan if attacked. Most cities that had RDD and IND response plans reported conducting exercises to validate the plans based on federal guidance.

Major cities varied widely in perceptions of their abilities to respond within the first 24 hours of RDD and IND attacks (early response). For example, all 27 cities were perceived by their emergency managers as being able to conduct at least a few of the early response activities after an RDD attack, such as treating casualties, with assistance from other jurisdictions but not federal assistance. Ten of those cities were perceived as not being able to conduct any of the response activities for an IND attack without federal assistance. GAO analysis found that these perceptions were not necessarily related to a city having RDD and IND response plans but rather related to their understanding of nuclear and radiological incidents and the capabilities needed for response according to information obtained from Federal Emergency Management Agency (FEMA) officials. GAO found limited federal planning guidance related to the early response capabilities needed by cities for the large RDD attack depicted in the national planning scenarios. Federal guidance may not be needed, according to FEMA officials, because they expect cities to address a more likely but smaller RDD attack—as they would a hazardous materials spill—with limited federal assistance. More federal planning guidance applicable to cities has been developed for IND response, but this guidance does not detail the early response capabilities needed by cities in relation to other sources of assistance. Without greater awareness of and additional federal guidance on the capabilities needed by cities for early response to these attacks, cities may not have the information they need to adequately prepare for and respond to them. This could lead to complications that result in greater loss of life and economic impacts.

Most emergency managers reported perceived needs for federal technical and resource assistance to support their cities' early response to RDD (19 of 27 cities) and IND (21 of 27 cities) attacks. However, GAO found that federal guidance on the type and timing of such assistance is not readily available or understood by all emergency managers. This condition could lead to a disjointed and untimely response that might increase the consequences of either kind of attack. Emergency managers also reported a need for improved procedures and more information that FEMA is addressing. In addition, most emergency managers reported their city needed federal funding to maintain current capabilities to respond to RDD and IND attacks. According to DHS guidance, response capabilities are developed through planning, training, equipping, and exercising, which are essential elements of an integrated, capability-based approach to preparedness.

ABBREVIATIONS

DOD	Department of Defense
DOE	Department of Energy
DHS	Department of Homeland Security
FEMA	Federal Emergency Management Agency
FIOP	Federal Interagency Operational Plan
HHS	Department of Health and Human Services
IND	improvised nuclear device

NNSA   National Nuclear Security Administration
RDD   radiological dispersal device
UASI   Urban Areas Security Initiative

September 30, 2013

The Honorable Thomas R. Carper
Chairman
Committee on Homeland Security and Governmental Affairs
United States Senate

Dear Mr. Chairman:

A terrorist attack in a major city using a weapon of mass destruction would result in not only the loss of life but also enormous psychological and economic impacts. Since the terrorist attacks of September 11, 2001, concerns have intensified over major cities' preparedness to respond to an attack using a radiological dispersal device (RDD)—a mechanism to deliberately release radioactive material in sufficient quantities to require protective actions—or an improvised nuclear device (IND)[1]—a weapon fabricated using fissile material that produces a nuclear explosion.[2] Urban centers of major cities are assumed to be preferred targets for a terrorist attack, and local governments, along with their states, would have primary responsibilities for early response—within the first 24 hours—until additional resources, if needed, arrive from the federal government.[3] To prepare to respond early to an RDD or IND attack, cities will need to understand the risks and plan to respond if an attack occurs. According to a 2012 National Science and Technology Council report,[4] the ability to prepare for such an attack and act decisively and appropriately in the first minutes and hours after an attack will require reliable information, capabilities, and tools to assist in planning and to effectively mitigate consequences. A disjointed or untimely response could put many additional lives at risk, increase economic consequences, and undermine the public's confidence in the federal, state, and local governments' ability to respond to such a crisis.

In March 2011, the President directed the Secretary of Homeland Security, Department of Homeland Security (DHS), to develop a national preparedness goal and design a national preparedness system to address the threats posing the greatest risk to the security of the nation, and to issue an annual national preparedness report.[5] The national preparedness goal defines the core capabilities necessary to prepare for specific types of incidents, including acts of terrorism, cyber attacks, pandemics, and catastrophic natural disasters.[6] In September 2011, DHS published the National Preparedness Goal,[7] which stated that all levels of government and the whole community should present and assess risks in a similar manner to provide a common understanding of the threats and hazards confronting the country. Consistent with the National Preparedness Goal, the information gathered during a risk assessment will also enable a prioritization of preparedness efforts and provide an opportunity to identify capability requirements across all levels of government and the private sector. In this context, an RDD or IND attack would pose both a threat prior to the incident and a hazard after detonation.

As directed by the President, the national preparedness system is intended to guide activities to achieve the national preparedness goal. Specifically, it is to provide guidance on the planning, organization, equipment, training, and exercises needed to develop and maintain domestic capabilities. The national preparedness system is to include a series of integrated national planning frameworks for five mission areas— prevention, protection, mitigation, response, and recovery—built on basic plans that support an all hazards approach to preparedness. The all hazards approach allows emergency planners at all government levels to address common operational functions in their basic plans instead of having unique plans for every type of hazard. Each national planning framework is directed to include guidance to support corresponding planning at other governmental levels, including cities. The directive called for the national preparedness system to include development of a Federal Interagency Operational Plan (FIOP) to support each of the five mission area planning frameworks, such as the one for the response mission area.[8] In November 2011, DHS published the National Preparedness System and has been working to implement this system.[9]

The directive also recognizes that the national planning frameworks could include supplements, called annexes, describing additional planning guidance for particular hazard scenarios. DHS has previously prepared guidance in 2006 on planning assumptions for major attacks and natural disasters, including RDD and IND attacks, as a reference to help planners at all levels of government identify the potential scope, magnitude, and complexity of these events.[10] DHS stated in this guidance that this was done to establish a range of response capabilities to facilitate preparedness planning and exercising these plans. The 2008 National Response Framework, under revision, already includes a nuclear and radiological incident annex. According to Federal Emergency Management Agency (FEMA) officials, the FIOPs will likely include operational details for most, if not all of the national planning framework annexes.

The President also directed that the national preparedness system be consistent with the previously developed National Incident Management System, which provides a systematic and coordinated all hazards approach to incident management across all levels of government.[11] The National Incident Management System sets forth a comprehensive national approach that recognizes that incidents typically begin and end locally and are managed on a daily basis at the lowest jurisdictional level. However, there are incidents in which successful management of operations will need the involvement of multiple jurisdictions, levels of government, functional agencies, and emergency responder disciplines. Effective response to an RDD or IND attack would require marshalling all available federal, state, and local resources to save lives and limit economic damage.

DHS has lead federal coordinating responsibility for attacks involving nuclear or radiological materials, including RDDs and INDs. FEMA, within DHS, has responsibility to reduce the loss of life and property, and protect the nation from all hazards, including terrorism. FEMA has a leadership role to coordinate the overall federal response to these attacks in close coordination with many other federal agencies and departments.[12] Among other agencies, these include the Department of Energy (DOE), Department of Defense (DOD), and the Department of Health and Human Services (HHS). Within DOE, the semiautonomous National Nuclear Security Administration (NNSA) would lead the early federal interagency response to characterize the nature and dispersal of radioactive material in the event of an RDD or IND attack. DOD may provide support in response to requests for assistance from DHS, other federal agencies, as well as state and local governments.[13] HHS would lead all federal public health and medical response to supplement state and local resources during a public health and medical disaster. In addition, the National Guard can provide governors with a wide array of response capabilities in detection/identification, search and rescue, patient decontamination, and medical care to relieve or augment first responders.

Since major cities are presumed to be preferred targets for terrorist attacks, you asked us to examine their concerns about RDD and IND attacks and how they perceive their ability to respond to them before federal assistance arrives. This report examines major cities' (1) assessment of the risks of RDD and

IND attacks and the extent to which they have developed plans for responding to them, (2) perceptions of their abilities to respond to RDD and IND attacks in the first 24 hours (early response), and (3) perceptions of their need for federal support in the early response to RDD and IND attacks.

To conduct this work, we developed a questionnaire for the directors of emergency management of 31 major cities that DHS considers at highest risk for a terrorist act in fiscal year 2012. We were able to contact an emergency manager to receive the questionnaire in 29 of the 31 cities.[14] We selected city emergency managers to receive the questionnaire because they are in the best position to provide a city-wide perspective on the level of preparedness to respond to RDD and IND attacks. Emergency managers from 27 of the 29 major cities that received our questionnaire responded for a response rate of 87 percent. This questionnaire asked city emergency managers to report on (1) how their city assessed the risk of RDD and IND attacks, and the availability of local response plans for these attacks; (2) their perceptions of their city's ability to respond within the first 24 hours (early response); and (3) their perceptions of the need for federal support to prepare for and respond to these attacks. In addition, we reviewed federal guidance documents and other relevant reports. We also interviewed emergency managers or first responders in seven major cities selected for their geographic location and population size, and visited with emergency management planners who participated in an interagency IND response planning effort in Chicago. We also interviewed FEMA and NNSA emergency management planners, DOE national laboratory officials, and subject matter experts. We conducted these interviews to obtain information on the availability of federal technical and response assistance, initiatives to improve information and procedures, and the availability of federal funding to support preparedness efforts by major cities. Appendix I provides a more detailed description of our objectives, scope, and methodology. A copy of our questionnaire is found in appendix II.

We conducted this performance audit from June 2012 to September 2013 in accordance with generally accepted government auditing standards. Those standards require that we plan and perform the audit to obtain sufficient, appropriate evidence to provide a reasonable basis for our findings and conclusions based on our audit objectives. We believe that the evidence obtained provides a reasonable basis for our findings and conclusions based on our audit objectives.

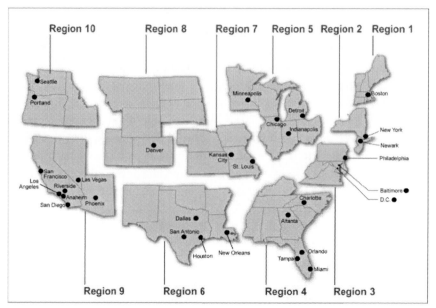

Source: Copyright © Corel Corp. All rights reserved (map); GAO.

Figure 1. Major Cities at High Risk for Terrorist Attack by FEMA Region.

BACKGROUND

Characteristics of RDD and IND Attacks

This section provides information on the characteristics of RDD and IND attacks, major cities considered at high risk of terrorist act, core capabilities for all hazards preparedness, and response planning and associated federal guidance in the national preparedness system.

A radiological attack is defined as an event or series of events leading to the deliberate release, or potential release into the environment, of radioactive materials in sufficient quantity to require consideration of protective actions. Such an act would probably be executed with no advance warning. The typical means of dispersing radioactive material in an RDD is through a conventional explosion. There is a wide range of possible consequences from an RDD incident depending on the type and size of the device and the extent of dispersal. According to FEMA officials, the most likely RDD attack would impact a small area and not result in acutely harmful radiation doses to exposed individuals but could result in latent effects increasing the risk of cancer to exposed individuals. In contrast, an IND attack would produce a nuclear explosion from fissile material, which releases extreme heat and powerful shock waves, and disperses radiation that would be lethal for a significant distance. It also produces radioactive fallout, which would deposit radioactive material over a large area. If the fission of the radioactive material is not achieved, the effects of the explosion may resemble the impacts of an RDD. A 2011 Congressional Research Service report states that the use of an RDD is more likely than an IND because the radioactive material to construct an RDD is more accessible, and it would be more difficult for a terrorist to make an IND.[15] In both cases, early response within the first hours includes initial actions to protect public health and welfare.

Major Cities Considered at High Risk of Terrorist Attack

In 2003, DHS established an Urban Areas Security Initiative program to allocate homeland security grants to enhance and sustain the capacity to prevent, protect against, mitigate, respond to, and recover from acts of terrorism in high density urban areas, particularly the urban centers. The program identifies these high density urban areas by their major city. For example, the Chicago area includes 3 states, 14 counties, and 10 principal cities. Figure 1 shows the 31 major cities in the Urban Areas Security Initiative program in fiscal year 2012 within the 10 FEMA regions.

Core Capabilities for All Hazards Preparedness

In the National Preparedness Goal, DHS identified core capabilities needed for each of the five national preparedness mission areas. These core capabilities are considered necessary for an all hazards, capability- based approach to preparedness planning across all levels of government, although each level of government does not have to possess all capabilities. The five mission areas have in common three core capabilities—planning, public information and warning, and operational coordination—in addition to other capabilities specific to each mission area. For the response mission area, there are 11 additional core capabilities, for a total of 14. In compiling the list of core response capabilities, DHS based them on those capabilities that would be needed to respond to a large earthquake, major hurricane, and a weapon of mass destruction attack. Table 1 describes the activities for each of the 14 core capabilities in the response mission area that DHS considers necessary to save lives, protect property, and meet basic human needs after a catastrophic incident, such as an RDD or IND attack.

Response Planning and Associated Federal Guidance

Under the national preparedness system, FEMA has issued guidance to help planners at all levels of government develop and maintain viable, all hazards emergency operations plans. This guidance describes how to develop and maintain emergency operations plans and how to implement these plans.[16] While the basic emergency operations plan is oriented around an all hazards approach, FEMA guidance states that special policies may be necessary to respond to catastrophic incidents, such as an RDD or IND attack. According to FEMA guidance, local governments have the discretion to address these attacks in specific plans that are annexed to a city's emergency operations plan, and the inclusion of these annexes will vary based on a jurisdiction's assessment of the risks it faces. DHS guidance establishing the national preparedness system recognizes that since local governments will focus their planning efforts on the more likely risks, federal planning must complement these planning efforts for low-probability, high-consequence risks, such as a terrorist attack using an RDD or IND.[17] DHS issued preliminary guidance for RDD and IND response planning to federal, state, and local governments in 2008, through a Federal Register announcement, that was followed in 2010 with additional federal guidance on responding to an IND attack.[18] Some professional organizations have also published guidance covering measures that state and local government should consider in responding to RDD and IND attacks.[19] Figure 2 illustrates the conceptual response planning framework, including possible nuclear or radiological attack annexes as supplements to all hazards operational or emergency operations plans supporting national preparedness.

Table 1. Activities Associated with Each Core Capability for the Response Mission Area

Core capability	Activities
Planning	Conduct a systematic process engaging the whole community, as appropriate, in the development of executable strategic, operational, and/or community-based approaches to meet defined objectives.
Public Information and Warning	Deliver coordinated, prompt, reliable, and actionable information to the whole community through the use of clear, consistent, accessible, and culturally and linguistically appropriate methods to effectively relay information regarding any threat or hazard and, as appropriate, the actions being taken and the assistance being made available.
Operational Coordination	Establish and maintain a unified and coordinated operational structure and process that appropriately integrates all critical stakeholders and supports the execution of core capabilities.
Critical Transportation	Provide transportation (including infrastructure access and accessible transportation services) for response priority objectives, including the evacuation of people and animals, and the delivery of vital response personnel, equipment, and services into the affected areas.
Environmental Response/Health and Safety	Ensure the availability of guidance and resources to address all hazards including hazardous materials, acts of terrorism, and natural disasters in support of the responder operations and the affected communities.
Fatality Management Services	Provide fatality management services, including body recovery and victim identification, working with state and local authorities to provide temporary mortuary solutions, sharing information with mass care services for the purpose of reunifying family members and caregivers with missing persons/remains, and providing counseling to the bereaved.
Infrastructure Systems	Stabilize critical infrastructure functions, minimize health and safety threats, and efficiently restore and revitalize systems and services to support a viable, resilient community.
Mass Care Services	Provide life-sustaining services to the affected population with a focus on hydration, feeding, and sheltering to those who have the most need, as well as support for reunifying families.

Table 1. (Continued)

Core capability	Activities
Mass Search and Rescue Operations	Deliver traditional and atypical search and rescue capabilities, including personnel, services, animals, and assets to survivors in need, with the goal of saving the greatest number of endangered lives in the shortest time possible.
On-scene Security and Protection	Ensure a safe and secure environment through law enforcement and related security and protection operations for people and communities located within affected areas and also for all traditional and atypical response personnel engaged in lifesaving and life-sustaining operations.
Operational Communications	Ensure the capacity for timely communications in support of security, situational awareness, and operations by any and all means available, among and between affected communities in the impact area and all response forces.
Public and Private Services and Resources	Provide essential public and private services and resources to the affected population and surrounding communities, to include emergency power to critical facilities, fuel support for emergency responders, and access to community staples (e.g., grocery stores, pharmacies, and banks) and fire and other first response services.
Public Health and Medical Services	Provide lifesaving medical treatment via emergency medical services and related operations and avoid additional disease and injury by providing targeted public health and medical support and products to all people in need within the affected area.
Situational Assessment	Provide all decision makers with decision-relevant information regarding the nature and extent of the hazard, any cascading effects, and the status of the response.

Source: DHS, National Preparedness Goal, September 2011.

MANY MAJOR CITIES ASSESSED THE RISK OF RDD AND IND ATTACKS AS LOWER THAN OTHER HAZARDS THEY FACE, AND FEW HAD DEVELOPED SPECIFIC RESPONSE PLANS

Many major city emergency managers, although not all, responded to our questionnaire that their city had assessed the risks of RDD and IND attacks and had ranked the risk of these attacks as lower than the risk of other hazards their city faces. The results of our questionnaire also show that fewer than half of the major cities that responded had developed specific RDD and IND response plans. Most of the major cities that reported having RDD and IND response plans also reported having conducted exercises to validate those plans.

Many of the Major Cities Assessed the Risk of RDD and IND Attacks as Lower than Other Hazards

Emergency managers of many of the major cities responding to our questionnaire reported that their city assessed the risk of RDD and IND attacks and ranked those risks as lower than other hazards their city faces. We asked emergency managers to refer to their city's most recently completed Hazard Identification and Vulnerability Assessment,[20] and report whether they assessed the risk of RDD or IND attacks and, if so, where those risks ranked relative to the other hazards assessed by their city, such as hurricanes, tornadoes, and flooding. All 27 cities responded to our question regarding their assessment of the risks of RDD and IND attacks. Three major cities reported that they had not completed a Hazard Identification and Vulnerability Assessment, or a similar assessment, and 6 cities reported that while they did have a recent assessment, they did not include either RDD or IND attacks in this assessment. Of the remaining 18 cities, 7 combined RDD and IND attacks into a single risk in their assessments, 9 assessed the risk of RDD and IND attacks separately, and 2 assessed the risk of an RDD attack but did not assess the risk of an IND attack. Of the 11 cities that assessed the risk of an RDD attack separately, 7 ranked the risk as lower than most or all other hazards their city faces. Of the 9 cities that separately assessed the risk of an IND attack, 7 ranked the risk as lower than most or all other hazards their city faces. In general, most cities that conducted a separate risk assessment for both

RDD and IND reported that the risk of an RDD attack was higher than the risk of an IND attack. Table 2 shows the approach taken by the major cities responding to our questionnaire for assessing the risks of RDD and IND attacks, as well as the percentage of cities for each approach that ranked these risks lower than most or all other hazards they face.

Fewer Than Half of Major Cities Have Specific Response Plans for RDD and IND Attacks

According to the responses to our questionnaire, fewer than half of the major cities have response plans[21] that specifically address RDD and IND attacks, although some emergency managers indicated that their city had these plans in development. Of the 27 major cities that responded to our questionnaire, 11 (41 percent) of the emergency managers reported that their city had completed RDD response plans, and 8 (30 percent) had completed IND response plans. Some emergency managers for cities that did not have specific RDD and IND response plans reported that they would rely on other plans in the event of such an attack, including their city's emergency operations plan or hazard management plan. Table 3 identifies the extent to which major cities have hazard-specific RDD or IND response plans.

Table 2. Radiological Dispersal Device (RDD) or Improvised Nuclear Device (IND) Attack Risk Assessment Approach for 27 Major Cities and the Percentage Ranking These Hazards as Lower Than Other Hazards They Face

Type of hazard assessed	Cities assessing the hazard as lower than most or all other hazards they face	
	Number	**Percentage**
RDD attack separately	7 of 11 cities that reported doing an assessment of an RDD attack[a]	64%
IND attack separately	7 of 9 cities that reported doing an assessment of an IND attack	78%
RDD/IND attacks combined	5 of 7 cities that reported doing an assessment of RDD/IND attacks combined	71%

Source: GAO questionnaire results.

[a] One of the 11 cities that separately assessed the risk of an RDD attack incorrectly skipped the question of where the risk of RDD attacks ranked relative to all other hazards their city faces.

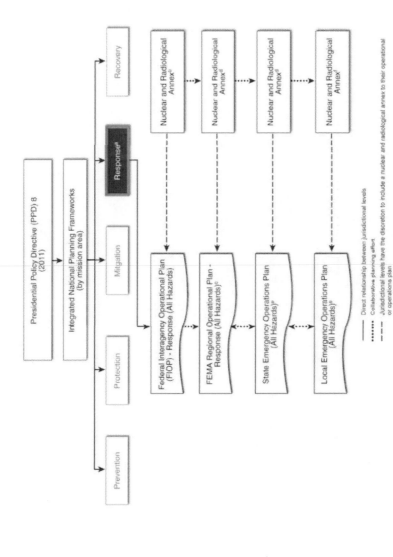

Source: GAO.

Note: An alternative to supplementing an all hazards plan with a nuclear and radiological annex to account for changes in objectives and tasks might be to amend the all hazards plan itself.

^a DHS issued its first *National Response Framework* in 2008 that included emergency support functions, incident annexes, and the partner guides. A new response framework is under development.

^b FEMA is considering the need to revise the existing nuclear and radiological incident annex to the *National Response Framework* as an annex to a forthcoming FIOPs for the response and recovery mission areas.

^c This plan is based on FEMA's *Regional Planning Guide*, which outlines the means to implement the planning process consistent with FEMA's *Comprehensive Preparedness Guide (CPG) 101*.

^d State governments have the option to develop specific plans that are annexed to their emergency operations plans based on their assessment of the hazard risk, such as a nuclear and radiological annex. As of 2012, all regional offices, states, and Urban Areas Security Initiative locations must use the Threat and Hazard Identification and Risk Assessment process.

^e This plan is based on FEMA's *Comprehensive Preparedness Guide (CPG) 101*.

^f Local governments have the option to develop specific plans that are annexed to their emergency operations plans based on their assessment of the hazard risk, such as a nuclear and radiological annex. Local governments often use the Hazard Identification and Vulnerability Assessment process to develop their Hazard Mitigation Plans.

Figure 2. Conceptual Response Planning Framework for Radiological Dispersal Device (RDD) and Improvised Nuclear Device (IND) Attacks within the National Preparedness System.

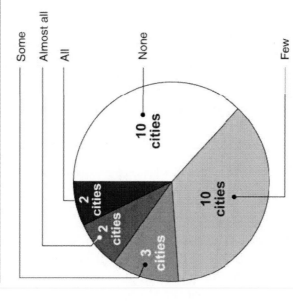

Radiological dispersal device

All
0 cities
None

Few — 5 cities

Some — 5 cities

7 cities

10 cities

Almost all

Improvised nuclear device

Some
Almost all
All

None — 10 cities

Few — 10 cities

2 cities

2 cities

3 cities

Source: GAO analysis of questionnaire data.

Note: Early response in an RDD or IND attacks refers to the abilities of major cities to respond to such an attack within the first 24 hours. The statements made by emergency managers of 27 cities regarding the response activities they would provide included mutual aid from their state, as well as surrounding jurisdictions, but not response assistance from the federal government.

Figure 3. Amount of Perceived Early Response Ability of 27 Major Cities for Radiological Dispersal Device (RDD) and Improvised Nuclear Device (IND) Attacks.

Table 3. Number and Percentage of 27 Major Cities with Specific Radiological Dispersal Device (RDD) or Improvised Nuclear Device (IND) Response Plans

Type of hazard	Hazard-specific plans completed	Hazard-specific plans in development	No hazard-specific plans completed or in development	Planning for this hazard is not-applicable
RDD	11 (41%)	6 (22%)	10 (37%)	0 (0%)
IND	8 (30%)	8 (30%)	10 (37%)	1 (3%)

Source: GAO questionnaire results.

Note: All 27 cities that responded to the questionnaire provided information on whether they had specific plans for RDD or IND attacks.

The questionnaire results regarding the number of cities with specific response plans for RDD and IND attacks are generally consistent with prior analyses conducted by FEMA. In 2010, FEMA conducted a national review of the contents of state and urban area emergency operations plans.[22] FEMA found that more than 80 percent of urban areas reported that their emergency operations plans were well-suited to meet the challenges presented during large-scale or catastrophic incidents; however, fewer than half expressed confidence that specific RDD and IND response plans annexed to their emergency operations plans were adequate to manage such attacks. Forty percent of the urban areas had confidence in their RDD response plans, with 10 percent providing no response. Thirty percent said they had confidence in their IND response plans, with 20 percent providing no response.

Most Major Cities That Have Specific RDD and IND Response Plans Have Also Exercised These Plans

Most emergency managers responding to our questionnaire who reported having specific RDD or IND response plans also reported having conducted exercises to validate those plans based on federal guidance. According to FEMA, a response plan should not be considered complete until exercises are conducted to validate it. Of the 11 cities that have specific RDD response plans, 9 of their emergency managers reported that their city had participated in RDD exercises from 2010 to 2012. Of the 8 cities that have specific IND response plans, 5 of their emergency managers reported that their city had participated in IND exercises over this same time period. These results are comparable to FEMA's 2010 national review of emergency operations plans that found that plans were frequently exercised. Specifically, 95 percent of all states and urban areas (including the major cities in our questionnaire) had conducted exercises using their basic plans, an increase from the previous review in 2006, and the response planning annexes subject to the most exercises included those involving the response to the release of hazardous materials, which can include the dispersal of radioactivity from RDD and IND attacks.

MAJOR CITIES VARY WIDELY IN PERCEPTIONS OF THEIR ABILITIES TO RESPOND WITHIN 24 HOURS OF RDD AND IND ATTACKS

Major city emergency managers responding to our questionnaire varied widely in their perception of their cities' abilities to respond within the first 24 hours (early response) to an RDD or IND attack. Limited DHS guidance exists that is applicable to major cities on the capabilities needed for early response to an RDD attack, but more such guidance exists for the early response to an IND attack. According to FEMA officials, the agency is considering developing additional guidance on nuclear and radiological incidents to be annexed to the forthcoming FIOPs for the response and recovery mission areas that may help guide the preparation of specific response plans to supplement the all hazards emergency operations plans of cities interested in doing so.

Major Cities Vary Widely in Perceptions of Their Ability to Respond within 24 Hours of RDD and IND Attacks, but Perceive More Ability to Respond to an RDD Attack

Our analysis of the questionnaire responses from major city emergency managers showed a wide variation in their perceptions regarding their cities' abilities to respond within the first 24 hours to the RDD or IND attack depicted in the National Planning Scenarios, but most perceived that their city has more ability to conduct the early response for an RDD attack than for an IND attack. To gather this information, we obtained the emergency managers' self-assessments of their cities' abilities for early response to the national planning scenarios for RDD and IND attacks, but we did not ask them to assess their level of ability for each of the 14 federal core response capabilities.[23] We also asked them to consider mutual aid from other jurisdictions in estimating their early response abilities, but not to consider assistance from federal sources. Our analysis of emergency manager responses showed a wide variation in perceived early response abilities across the major cities. For example, 7 of 27 cities were perceived by their emergency managers as being able to conduct all of the activities needed for early response to an RDD attack without federal assistance—such as treating casualties—while 2 cities were perceived as being able to conduct all of the activities needed for an IND attack, without federal assistance. Moreover, all cities were perceived by their emergency managers as being able to conduct at least a few early response activities for an RDD attack, while 10 cities were perceived as not being able to conduct any early response activities for an IND attack. Overall, our analysis concluded that more emergency managers perceived that their city was able to conduct some, almost all, or all of the early response activities needed for an RDD attack (22 of 27 cities) compared with an IND attack (7 of 27 cities). Ten major cities reported not having any ability to conduct the early response after an IND attack, even considering assistance from the surrounding jurisdictions and their states, which would suggest a high expectation for federal assistance during early response. For RDD, emergency managers from 20 major cities reported perceiving that their city was not able to conduct all of the necessary early response activities, which may also suggest some expectation for federal assistance. Figure 3 shows the distribution of major cities among five categories of early response activities following an RDD or IND attack based on emergency manager perceptions of their city's early response abilities including mutual aid from other jurisdiction but not federal assistance.

The wide variation among emergency manager perceptions of their cities' abilities to conduct the early response to RDD and IND attacks is not necessarily related to whether or not a city had specific response plans. Our analysis found that 10 of the 17 major cities perceived by their emergency managers as being able to conduct all or almost all the necessary response activities for an RDD attack did not have specific RDD response plans. For IND attacks, three of the four major city perceived by their emergency managers as able conduct all or almost all of the necessary response activities for an IND attack did not have specific IND response plans. Regarding the wide differences in emergency managers' perceptions of their cities' abilities to respond, FEMA officials told us that some cities will tend to overestimate the risks of an RDD attack due to their lack of understanding about dispersed radioactive material and underestimate their actual abilities to conduct responses across the federal core response capabilities. They told us that cities in states with nuclear power plants are likely to have a greater understanding of the possible effects of a radiological attack and thus might be able to assess the risks and their cities' abilities to respond better than other cities. These cities would have access to state technical and resource assistance developed and exercised to respond to a radiological dispersal incident at a nuclear power plant, which would have some characteristics of the dispersal of radioactive material by an RDD. Moreover, FEMA officials told us that cities closer to federal offices and facilities tend to have more interaction with FEMA and NNSA subject matter experts and are likely to have a greater understanding of the nature of an RDD attack. In regard to IND attacks, FEMA officials told us that they would expect that emergency managers would claim that such an attack would overwhelm their city response resources and that their city would need federal assistance across most federal core response capabilities.

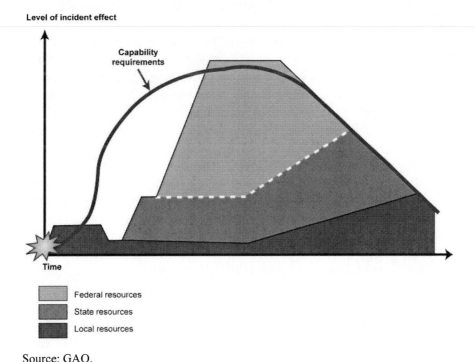

Source: GAO.

Figure 4. Anticipated Capability Requirements by Response Time.

Limited Federal Guidance Available on Early Response Capabilities Needed by Major Cities for RDD Attacks, but More Available for IND Attacks

DHS has provided limited guidance on the early response capabilities needed by cities for a large RDD attack based on the planning assumptions contained in the National Planning Scenarios, but more such guidance exists for the IND attack substantially based on the planning assumptions contained in the National Planning Scenarios. DHS has identified the core capabilities needed to respond to any catastrophic incident but generally not the specific capabilities needed by cities for early response to these attacks.[24] DHS guidance contained in an annex to the 2008 National Response Framework[25] states that an RDD or IND attack directed at a major city can have consequences that overwhelm the capabilities of state and local governments and may also seriously challenge existing federal response capabilities. In regard to RDD response, this DHS guidance states that major cities should be able to respond to small radiological releases with only occasional federal assistance but does not address the large RDD attack depicted in the National Planning Scenarios. According to FEMA and NNSA officials, additional federal guidance may not be necessary because they expect major cities to have the abilities to respond to a more likely smaller scale RDD attack than the large RDD attack, as they would a hazardous materials spill. If needed, the federal response to a hazardous materials release is described in an emergency support function covering oil and hazardous materials releases that is annexed to the National Response Framework.[26] DHS has also issued guidance on protective actions that should be taken at various phases of response, including early response to the dispersal of radioactive materials, such in an RDD attack.[27] However, the only detailed planning assumptions in current federal guidance for an RDD attack are those in the National Planning Scenarios and this is for a large RDD attack.[28] DHS has not provided guidance on the early response capabilities needed by major cities for such an attack. According to NNSA officials, cities are likely to reach out for federal support in the case of either a large or small-scale RDD attack due to the rarity of the event and the high profile of any radiological emergency.

The federal government has issued more guidance pertaining to early response to an IND attack substantially based on the National Planning Scenario.[29] In 2009, DHS issued an interim concept of operations plan for the federal response to the IND attack.[30] This federal operations plan states that the federal priority in the first 24 hours is to assist in saving lives and reducing casualties, while providing advice to those in the incident area to shelter in the nearest structure and listen for instructions from authorities. This federal operations plan also directs the states and local governments to delineate control zones, coordinate evacuations, make shelter-in-place decisions, issue protective action recommendations, initiate decontamination procedures, and use the National Guard to assist with environmental monitoring, but it provides limited information on the capabilities needed to complete these actions. In 2010, a federal interagency task force issued planning guidance to all levels of government that expanded on the 2008 DHS planning guidance by addressing gaps in IND response, expanding the discussion of needed capabilities, and examining other IND scenarios beyond the one identified in the National Planning Scenario.[31] This 2010 guidance presents general background information that builds a foundation for specific planning recommendations on response to an IND attack during the first 24 to 72 hours prior to the arrival of significant federal resources. This guidance states that other recommendations would be forthcoming, such as for establishing critical communications among first responders. This guidance recognizes that response planning must be done on a city- specific basis using city-specific impact assessments.[32] However, this guidance also points out that response to an IND will largely be provided from neighboring jurisdictions, which would require advanced planning to establish mutual aid and response protocols. Notwithstanding the specific planning recommendations, the 2010 planning guidance does not detail the early response capabilities needed by major cities to an IND attack in relation to other sources of assistance. Without greater awareness of and additional federal guidance on the capabilities needed by cities for early response to both RDD and IND attacks, cities may not have the information they need to adequately prepare for and respond to them. Any gaps in response capabilities could lead to complications that result in greater loss of life and economic impacts. Figure 4 provides a simple illustration of the capability requirements for increasing levels of incident effects, with an IND attack likely to be the highest level of incident effect.[33]

FEMA Is Considering Developing Additional Guidance for Response to RDD and IND Attacks That May Help Guide Development of Specific Response Plans by Major Cities

FEMA is considering the need to develop a nuclear and radiological annex, as depicted in figure 2, to help guide federal response activities and possibly assist in the development of specific response plans for RDD and IND attacks as supplements to city emergency operations plans. This federal nuclear and radiological annex would be attached to the forthcoming FIOPs—currently under review for approval—for the all hazards planning framework for the response and recovery mission areas. FEMA officials told us that a nuclear and radiological annex may be needed to supplement these FIOPs because their all hazards orientation would not address several unique requirements and concepts of operations specifically tailored to the needs for nuclear and radiological incidents. The need for such an annex is also supported by a 2012 DHS report that found the response and recovery needs after a radiological attack differ from traditional all hazards incidents due to the need for decontamination activities, heightened public anxiety, long-term risk management, and substantial disruption to citizen's lives and the economy.[34] FEMA officials said that if they decide to develop a nuclear and radiological annex it could help guide adjustments to FEMA regional operational plans. They also told us that these adjustments to the regional operational plans may help encourage major cities in FEMA regions to develop annexes to their all hazards emergency operations plans covering specific RDD and IND response plans.

FEMA has not determined what it might include in the nuclear and radiological annex or how to address RDD and IND response planning. FEMA officials told us that this annex is expected to address RDD and IND attacks, as well as a broader spectrum of radiological dispersal incidents, such as nuclear power plant accidents. According to FEMA guidance, separate hazards can be grouped under a more general category, such as terrorist acts, but FEMA recognizes that problems can arise that will affect subsequent analysis when grouping hazards with a wide range of consequences under a single category, such as might be the case with RDD and IND attacks.[35] FEMA officials provided information to compare the characteristics of RDD and IND attacks, as shown in table 4. One of the characteristics is the magnitude of the RDD and IND attacks. FEMA officials told us that if they decided to develop the nuclear and radiological annex, they would also consider the need to clarify the planning assumptions for these incidents, particularly the RDD attack scenario.

An additional FEMA consideration in developing the nuclear and radiological annex to the FIOPs is the information recently gained from the agency's participation in a multigovernmental initiative to develop an IND regional operations plan for Chicago, which is intended to guide development of other regionally based IND operations plans.[36] For example, FEMA found that the development of this IND regional operations plan provided information on needed early response capabilities, coordination of stakeholder groups, the type and timing of federal assistance, and the level of effort to complete the plan. The IND planning team determined that the most feasible course of action to save the greatest number of lives during early response involved concentrating on a limited number of activities around public information and warning, operational coordination and communications, on-scene security and protection, situational assessment, and shelter-in-place and evacuation.

These activities are covered by 7 of the 14 federal core response capabilities in the national preparedness goal. In addition, IND planning team members told us that the planning effort gave them a greater appreciation of the communication and coordination activities needed across stakeholder groups to respond to an IND attack. The planning effort involved more than 300 local, state, and federal emergency management offices and private entities. Moreover, the IND planning team was able to develop a detailed spreadsheet containing the type and timing of assistance that might be available and needed—at the three response phases—for an IND attack on Chicago. The development of the plan has taken time and substantial funding. The IND planning process has been under way since 2010, costing about $7.6 million, as of 2012, when the plan was completed. This cost includes the project work of the city, the state of Illinois, neighboring states, and federal agencies that contributed to the development of the overall plan.

As a result of the IND planning effort in Chicago, FEMA officials told us that they plan to use the information gained to assist other major cities seeking to develop similar operations plans with regional partners. FEMA officials told us that they also plan to undertake this planning initiative in Boston, the District of Columbia, and Houston during fiscal year 2013, with planning initiatives in Los Angeles, New York and Philadelphia to follow. In addition, FEMA officials told us that they plan to look for geographic and infrastructure similarities, such as common building structures and transportation systems in each region in order to expedite the planning process and reduce planning costs for other cities in a region. FEMA's Response Planning Division has allocated about $3.8 million for IND planning activities for fiscal year 2013. FEMA officials also told us that they thought that an IND response plan would be sufficient to address most of the response needs after an RDD attack as well.

Table 4. Comparison of Characteristics of Radiological Dispersal Device (RDD) and Improvised Nuclear Device (IND) Attacks

Categories	RDD characteristics	IND characteristics
Magnitude	Small scale destruction with wide range of possible magnitudes across city blocks with few deaths	Large-scale destruction affecting the entire metropolitan area with thousands of deaths
Time sensitivity	Right early decisions can reduce social and economic impacts	Right early decisions can save lives
Radioactive exposure risk	Limited number of people exposed to higher doses of radiation in various ways depending on the radioactive material	Large number of people having acute exposure in blast zone with widespread exposure to significant and/or lethal levels of radiation primarily downwind from fallout through gross exposure
Immediate health effects	Possible latent effects from radiation exposure	Immediate acute and latent effects from radiation exposure
Protective Actions	Avoid surfaces that have been contaminated	Shelter in buildings that have higher protection from radiation exposure

Source: GAO from FEMA information.

MOST MAJOR CITIES EXPRESSED NEED FOR FEDERAL SUPPORT FOR EARLY RESPONSE TO RDD AND IND ATTACKS

Emergency managers of major cities responding to our questionnaire reported varying levels of need for federal support in early response to RDD and IND attacks in the form of technical and resource assistance, procedures and information for early response activities, and preparedness funding. Emergency managers identified a number of areas for federal technical and resource assistance, but we found limitations in the federal guidance applicable to major cities on the type and timing of this assistance. Emergency managers of major cities also reported the need for federal government research that could improve procedures and information for their early response to RDD and IND attacks. DHS has supported working groups of subject matter experts to help mitigate shortcomings in response capabilities for IND attacks, which may have applications for improving RDD response capabilities. In addition, emergency managers reported that a decrease in federal funding would affect their abilities to conduct early response to RDD and IND attacks.

Major Cities Reported Need for Guidance on the Type and Timing of Federal Technical and Resource Assistance for Early Response to RDD and IND Attacks

Most emergency managers from major cities responding to our questionnaire reported that they need federal technical and resource assistance to support their early response to RDD and IND attacks, but federal guidance on the type and timing of this assistance is not found in a single document and may not be well understood by emergency managers. Nineteen of 27 emergency managers perceive a need for federal technical and resource assistance for early response to an RDD attack, and 21 of them perceive a need for this assistance in early response to an IND attack. Our analysis of questionnaire responses determined that of the 14 core response capabilities, emergency managers indicated that the capability most needing federal technical and resource assistance for both RDD and IND attacks (11 of 27 cities each) was situational assessment. Situational assessment provides decision makers with technical information such as the nature and extent of the hazard, its cascading effects, and the status of the response. For RDD attacks, after situational assessment, the emergency managers' next most frequently cited federal assistance needs were the following:

- public health and medical services (8 of 27 cities),
- operational coordination (5 of 27 cities), and
- on-scene security and protection (5 of 27 cities).[37]

For IND attacks, after situational assessment, the emergency managers' next most frequently cited federal assistance needs were as follows:

- on-scene security and protection (5 of 27 cities), and
- public health and medical services (5 of 27 cities).

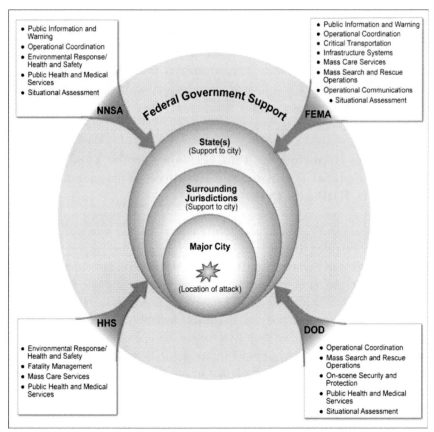

Source: GAO.

Note: This figure includes the four major agencies (DOE/NNSA, DHS/FEMA, HHS, and DOD) that would have primary responsibility for providing technical and resource assistance to a major city within the first 24 hours after an IND attack, although other federal agencies may be present. The need for core response capabilities from the federal government may differ for an RDD attack. This figure is based on our review of documents, such as DHS, Emergency Support Functions Annex to the National Response Framework (2008), DHS, Federal Interagency Improvised Nuclear Devices Concept of Operations Plan (2009), FEMA, IND Regional Operations Plan for Chicago (2012), and interviews with FEMA and NNSA officials.

Figure 5. Anticipated Federal Technical and Resource Support for Core Capabilities Necessary for a Major City Early Response to an Improvised Nuclear Device (IND) Attack.

We also obtained several responses from emergency managers regarding actions, such as planning, that the federal government should take to help sustain and improve early response capabilities. For example, one emergency manager commented that integrated RDD and IND plans of local, state, and federal government roles and responsibilities are nonexistent. Another emergency manager stated that that the federal government should provide a model RDD and IND response plan and templates to assist local jurisdictions' efforts.

The type and timing of federal assistance to major cities during the early response to an RDD or IND attack may not be well understood by all major city emergency managers, even though some guidance is available but in different documents. For example, in 2008, DHS issued guidance on federal agency responsibilities for responding to incidents involving the release of nuclear, radiological, and hazardous materials in the National Response Framework, and introduced the concept of phases of response in planning guidance for RDD and IND attacks. However, these and other guidance documents do not contain complete information on the type and timing of federal technical and resource assistance by response phases. For RDD attacks, DHS has not provided specific operational guidance on the type and timing of federal assistance that might be made available to cities for early response, although some information is available in an emergency support function annex to the National Response Framework. For IND attacks, DHS identified the technical and resource activities that federal agencies could provide to respond to an IND attack in a 2009 federal interim concept of operations plan and more recently in the 2012 IND regional operations plan for Chicago. In addition, federal agencies have provided various descriptions of the type and timing of the federal assistance that might be available on their websites. However, FEMA officials told us that the type and timing of the federal response would depend on the proximity of the city to federal offices. Confusion over the type and timing of assistance, such as federal assistance in the case of an IND attack, could produce a disjointed and untimely early response to the attack that might increase its consequences.

Based on information from a variety of sources, some of which may not be readily available to major cities, we developed an illustration of the federal agencies most likely to assist these cities during early response with activities associated with the core capabilities they claim they can support after an IND attack. While other federal agencies are involved through their emergency support functions under the National Response Framework, a senior FEMA official told us that the four federal agencies we identified in figure 5 would be the most involved during the first 24 hours after an IND attack. Figure 5 provides an illustration of the federal technical and resource support for the core capabilities necessary for major city early response to an IND attack.

Major Cities Reported Need for Improved Procedures and Information for Early Response to RDD and IND Attacks

Most emergency managers responding to our questionnaire indicated that their cities perceive a need for federal government research that could improve procedures or information for their early response to RDD and IND attacks. Using DHS guidance, we developed a list of 10 topic areas for federal government research initiatives that could improve procedures or information used by cities during the first 24 hours after the detonation of an RDD or IND.[38] We asked emergency managers for their opinions on how much impact, if any, each topic area might have on improving their city's capability for early response to an RDD or IND attack. For example, emergency managers from two-thirds of the major cities (18 of 27 cities) identified communicating a sheltering-in-place strategy to the public and communicating potential impacts of radiation exposure to the public as the topic areas having the highest impact. Figure 6 shows emergency managers' responses identifying the topic areas their city considers important for improving procedures or information necessary for early response to RDD and IND attacks.

We compared the emergency managers' responses on the impact that improved procedures and information might have on their city's early response to RDD and IND attacks with the research initiatives being considered by six FEMA IND focus working groups to determine if they align. FEMA has established these working groups of subject matter experts to mitigate shortcomings in response capabilities for an IND attack, such as clarifying responsibilities and coordinating efforts among government levels and federal agencies.[39] We found that the areas addressed by the working groups through their initiatives are generally the same as those topic areas emergency managers reported as having a high impact on procedures and information needed for early response to an RDD and IND attack.

FEMA does not have current plans to identify or attempt to fill potential gaps in capabilities for early response specifically to an RDD attack. However, IND focus area working group experts and a senior FEMA official told us that their efforts to fill gaps in IND capabilities and all hazards plans would have application for other catastrophic hazards, including RDD attacks. For example, they told us that RDD and IND attacks share some common attributes, such as (1) the release of radiological materials, (2) the need for decontamination and radiation treatment, and (3) prioritization of response resources and personnel based on ethical, philosophical, legal, and practical decision tools. In addition, both types of attacks also require communication of consistent information about radiation effects on general health outcomes and protective measures. Further, NNSA officials told us they also have several programs that might apply to RDD, as well as IND planning and capability enhancements.

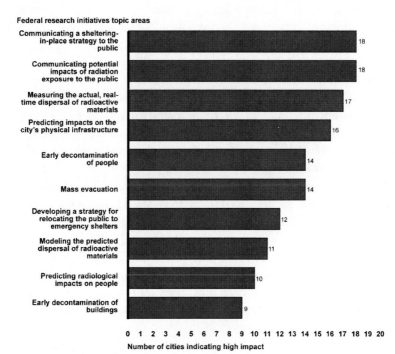

Source: GAO content analysis of questionnaire responses.

Note: GAO received questionnaire responses from emergency managers of 27 major cities: Anaheim, Baltimore, Boston, Charlotte, Chicago, Dallas, Denver, Detroit, Houston, Indianapolis, Kansas City, Las Vegas, Los Angeles, Miami, Minneapolis, New Orleans, New York City, Orlando, Philadelphia, Portland, Riverside, San Diego, San Francisco, Seattle, St. Louis, Tampa, and the District of Columbia.

Figure 6. Federal Radiological Dispersal Device (RDD) or Improvised Nuclear Device (IND) Response Topic Areas Identified by Major City Emergency Managers as Needed to Improve Early Response Capabilities.

Major Cities See Need for Federal Funding to Maintain Early Response to RDD and IND Attacks

Most emergency managers responding to our questionnaire indicated that their cities need federal funding to maintain current early response capabilities to an RDD or IND attack. Almost all emergency managers (24 of 27 cities for RDD and 23 of 27 cities for IND) indicated that their city needs federal funding to maintain current early response capabilities. According to the 2008 National Response Framework, response capabilities are developed within the national preparedness system through effective planning, coordinating, training, equipping, and exercising activities. These activities are essential elements of an integrated, capability-based approach to preparedness. Emergency managers reported that a decrease in federal funding would affect the degree to which each of these activities builds the capabilities needed for early response to an RDD or IND attack. Our analysis of questionnaire results indicated that about a third of 27 cities identified equipment, training, and planning activities important to the capabilities that would be most affected by a decrease in federal preparedness funding, with fewer cities indicating that coordination and exercising would be affected.

Federal funding to support preparedness against terrorist attacks and other catastrophic incidents such as RDD and IND attacks currently comes from seven DHS grant programs.[40] In fiscal year 2013, DHS allocated more than $1.5 billion for these seven grant programs, but officials in charge of these programs were unable to determine how much of the funding was used by major cities to improve early RDD and IND response capabilities.[41] Two of the DHS grant programs that have been most relevant to response preparation for an RDD or IND attack are the Homeland Security Grant Program and the temporary (fiscal years 2008 to 2011) Regional Catastrophic Planning Grant Program. In fiscal year 2013, DHS allocated more than $968 million to the Homeland Security Grant Program, and more than half (roughly $560 million) was allocated to Urban Areas Security Initiative grants, a portion of which goes to law enforcement terrorism prevention activities. The Regional Catastrophic Planning Grant Program awarded $14 million in grants in fiscal year 2011, the last year it made awards, to support regional planning efforts to address catastrophic incidents.[42] For example, these funds were used by New York and New Jersey to develop RDD and IND response plans and were also combined with other federal funding to support development of the IND regional operations plan for Chicago. According to members of the IND planning team for Chicago, the Regional Catastrophic Planning Grant Program provided the funding to bring together the many stakeholder groups that would be involved in responding to an IND attack and, without continued funding, it would be difficult to maintain the same level of collaboration. Appendix III provides a detailed breakdown of the seven federal grant programs for fiscal year 2013.

CONCLUSION

DHS has recognized that the early response to catastrophic incidents such as an RDD or IND attack on a major city is critical and has to come first from the city and surrounding jurisdictions. While cities are assumed to be preferred targets for an RDD or IND attack, in response to our questionnaire, many emergency managers indicated that their cities ranked the risk of these attacks as lower than other hazards their cities face, and fewer than half of the cities have specific response plans for such attacks. City emergency managers rely on federal guidance to prepare all hazards emergency operations plans and also specific response plans for hazards of concern that can be annexed to these emergency operations plans at the discretion of the city. However, we found limitations in the federal planning guidance applicable to the early response capabilities needed by cities for an RDD attack of the size depicted in the National Planning Scenarios. More federal planning guidance applicable to major cities has been developed for IND response, primarily based on the event depicted in the National Planning Scenarios, but this guidance does not detail the early response capabilities needed by major cities in relation to other sources of assistance. Perceptions of emergency managers varied widely on their cities' abilities to conduct the activities needed for early response to the type of RDD attacks described in the National Planning Scenarios—with assistance from surrounding jurisdictions but not the federal government—from being able to conduct all activities for early response to being able to conduct few early response activities. Less variation was evident for perceived early response abilities to an IND attack—considering this same source of assistance—with many cities indicating that such an attack would overwhelm their response abilities. Most cities indicated the need for federal technical and resource assistance—among other areas of federal support—for early response to RDD and IND attacks, but we found that complete guidance on the type and timing of this assistance is not readily available in a single document and is not well understood by all major city emergency managers. Any confusion over the type and timing of federal assistance could produce a disjointed and untimely early response to an attack that might increase its consequences. Without greater awareness of existing federal guidance and continued actions to close gaps in the guidance applicable to cities' early response to RDD and IND attacks, some cities may not have the information they need to adequately prepare for and respond to them. Lack of adequate response planning could lead to complications that result in greater loss of life and economic impacts.

RECOMMENDATION FOR EXECUTIVE ACTION

To provide assistance to major cities in planning for early response to RDD and IND attacks, we recommend that the Secretary of Homeland Security direct the Administrator for the Federal Emergency Management Agency to promote greater awareness of existing federal guidance and develop additional guidance where appropriate to clarify the capabilities needed by cities for these attacks, including the planning assumptions for an RDD attack and the type and timing of federal assistance for early response.

AGENCY COMMENTS AND OUR EVALUATION

We provided a draft of this report to DHS and to DOE through NNSA for review and comment. DHS did not concur with our recommendation and provided written comments. In addition, in an e-mail received August 27, 2013, the Director, Audit Coordination and Internal Affairs Office of Management and Budget (NA- MB-1.1) for NNSA stated that as the recommendations in the report are directed to DHS and FEMA, NNSA would not be preparing a formal response. DHS and NNSA provided technical comments, which we incorporated as appropriate.

In the comment letter, DHS states that FEMA program officials and subject matter experts are concerned that our survey may have resulted in the receipt of skewed data and information that affected our analysis and conclusions. For example, the letter stated that some respondents may have believed that an IND/RDD event would or could be fully handled at the local level and therefore provided inputs partial toward taking on an inordinate level of responsibility. They also stated that our recommendation runs contrary to the survey results which illustrate a trend of grouping RDD and IND attacks for analysis and planning. We disagree. Our questionnaire explicitly asked city emergency managers to consider response assistance from surrounding jurisdictions in their assessment of response abilities, and only exclude federal assistance. In this way, we were able to isolate the perceived need for federal support, which we found for technical and resource assistance, improved procedures and information, and funding. Further, emergency managers did not provide trend information through their questionnaire responses on assessing RDD and IND risks, and cities more often separated the assessment of RDD and IND risks than combined them as DHS indicated in its comment letter. In addition, we took a number of steps to develop the questionnaire and to identify the best source for a response. For example, we conducted extensive pretesting and obtained comments on a draft questionnaire from officials at FEMA's National Preparedness Assessment Division. We also determined that city emergency managers were in the best position to provide a city-wide perspective on this issue, but we allowed them to seek advice from other city officials as necessary.

In its comment letter, DHS stated that neither the department nor FEMA believes that our recommendation that FEMA develop additional guidance in a single document to clarify the capabilities needed by cities for these attacks, including the planning assumptions for an RDD attack and addressing the type and timing of federal assistance for early response takes into sufficient account advances made to the preparedness system. In addition, the comment letter states that FEMA program officials and subject matter experts believe the recommendation does not align with our survey results or all-hazard risk management for worst case catastrophic scenarios. It also states that FEMA has concerns with the report's characterization of the nation's ability to respond to a nuclear and/or radiological attack. Furthermore, the letter states that additional RDD response guidance in a single document would be counterproductive to the existing planning and guidance structure for IND and all hazards incidents. As we note in the report, FEMA is already considering development of a nuclear and radiological incident annex to the FIOPs for the response and recovery mission areas based on the recognition that the all hazards approach may be insufficient to cover the unique response needs for nuclear and radiological incidents. While our recommendation did not specify how FEMA should provide this additional guidance, we have added language to the recommendation to clarify that that we are not recommending a single guidance document to cover only RDD response. In addition, to address the DHS/FEMA concern that city emergency managers may not be fully informed about available guidance, we added language to the recommendation for FEMA to promote greater awareness of existing federal guidance.

More generally, DHS' comment letter states that FEMA officials do not believe we provided adequate context for the National Preparedness System as defined by Presidential Policy Directive 8, which may cause confusion for cold readers not familiar with how the directive has been implemented. In addition, the comment letter states that the operational frameworks, structures, and ongoing efforts that have been developed in support of the directive's comprehensive approach to national response are not fully outlined in the report; specifically, the letter states that the Nuclear and Radiological Incident Annex to the National Response Framework and Emergency Support Functions as the nation's coordinating structures are not accurately portrayed and cites figure 5 as an inaccurate and misleading depiction of the federal response for an IND/RDD event. While the purpose of this report was not to conduct a detailed assessment of federal guidance or implementation of the directive, we added additional information about FEMA's leadership role in coordinating the federal response to nuclear and radiological incidents within the context of the National Response Framework and its efforts to develop IND response planning guidance. We also added that the illustration in figure 5 of federal agency support for core response capabilities that might be available to cities during the first 24 hours after an IND attack does not include all federal agencies' activities but only those four agencies confirmed by a senior FEMA official as being most present during this time period.

Sincerely yours,

David C. Trimble
Director, Natural Resources and Environment

APPENDIX I: OBJECTIVES, SCOPE, AND METHODOLOGY

In our review, we examined major cities' (1) assessment of the risks of RDD and IND attacks and the extent to which they have developed plans for responding to them, (2) perceptions of their abilities to respond to RDD and IND attacks in the first 24 hours (early response), and (3) perceptions of their need for federal support in the early response to RDD and IND attacks. To address these questions we sent a questionnaire to major city emergency managers, and we conducted interviews with outside experts and federal, state, and local officials.

To gather information from major U.S. cities relevant to all three of our objectives, we developed a questionnaire for the directors of emergency management for each of the 31 major cities that were in the Urban Areas Security Initiative (UASI) program in fiscal year 2012.[43] We chose the major cities within each UASI region because in our document review, as well as in interviews with the Federal Emergency Management Agency (FEMA), UASI regions were identified as higher risk jurisdictions for terrorist acts, including those using RDDs or INDs.[44] As FEMA guidance states that local jurisdictions should plan and develop capabilities to respond to incidents based on risk, these jurisdictions are in need of developing plans and preparing for the response to RDD and IND attacks. Each of the 31 UASI locations covers a large metropolitan area that includes many local governments. For example, the Chicago UASI includes 3 states, 14 counties, and 10 principal cities. It did not serve our purpose to send the questionnaire directly through the UASI structure itself as the number of jurisdictions involved could introduce issues of reliability in the answers, as well as consistency in terms of the process used by each UASI to fill out our questionnaire. FEMA officials told us that the largest metropolitan area within each UASI constitutes the area at the highest risk for attack in each jurisdiction. In addition, we selected city emergency managers to receive the questionnaire because they were in the best position to provide a city-wide perspective on the level of preparedness to respond to RDD and IND attacks. Therefore, we chose to send questionnaires to only the emergency managers of these large metropolitan areas. The emergency management offices in Atlanta and Newark did not respond to our contact attempts, so we sent out questionnaires to the 29 cities that did reply. In developing our questionnaire, we developed questions that addressed all three of the report objectives and had these reviewed both internally, as well as by staff of FEMA's National Preparedness Assessment Division. We conducted seven cognitive pretests with emergency management officials and first responders from major cities selected for their geographic location and population size in order to minimize errors that might occur from respondents who interpreted our questions differently than we intended. During these pretests, we also interviewed these emergency management officials and first responders to gain additional context regarding their city's preparedness for responding to either an RDD or IND attack.

The questionnaire was implemented as a self-administered Microsoft Word form e-mailed to respondents. We sent e-mail notifications to emergency managers beginning on December 11, 2012.[45] We then sent the questionnaire and a cover e-mail to officials on December 12, 2012, and asked them to fill in the questionnaire form and e-mail it back to us within 3 weeks. To encourage emergency managers to complete the questionnaire, we sent e-mail reminders and a replacement questionnaire to nonrespondents approximately 1 week after, and again 3 weeks after, the initial questionnaire was distributed. We also made follow-up phone calls to nonrespondents from January 24, 2013, to February 8, 2013. We closed the questionnaire on February 20, 2013. We received 27 completed questionnaires for an overall response rate of 87 percent— Phoenix and San Antonio did not return the questionnaire. Because we attempted to collect data from each of the UASI major cities rather than a sample of major cities, there was no sampling error. However, the practical difficulties of conducting any questionnaire may introduce errors, commonly referred to as nonsampling errors. For example, differences in how a particular question is interpreted, the sources of information available to respondents, how the responses were processed and analyzed, or the types of people who do not respond can influence the accuracy of the questionnaire results. We took steps in the development of the questionnaire, the data collection, and the data analysis to minimize these nonsampling errors and help ensure the accuracy of the answers that were obtained. For example, a GAO social science questionnaire specialist designed the questionnaire, in collaboration with GAO staff with subject matter expertise. The draft questionnaire was pretested to ensure that questions were relevant, clearly stated, and easy to comprehend. The questionnaire was also reviewed by external experts and a second GAO questionnaire specialist. Data were electronically extracted from the Microsoft Word form questionnaires into a comma-delimited file that was then imported into a statistical program for analyses. No manual data entry was performed, thereby removing an additional potential source of error. We examined the questionnaire results and performed computer analyses to identify inconsistencies and other indications of error and addressed such issues as were necessary. Additionally, we contacted respondents to clarify ambiguous responses when necessary. Quantitative data analyses and the compilation of open- ended responses were conducted by the first GAO questionnaire specialist using statistical software and working directly with GAO staff with subject matter expertise. An independent GAO data analyst checked the statistical computer programs for accuracy.

Responses to closed-ended (e.g., Yes/No) questions were summarized as standard descriptive statistics. Responses to open-ended (i.e., narrative) questions were analyzed through content analysis. In conducting the content analysis, one GAO analyst reviewed each open- ended response from each emergency manager to identify recurring themes. Using the identified themes, the analyst then developed categories for coding the responses. A second GAO analyst reviewed the responses from each emergency manager and reviewed the first analyst's themes and categories to reach concurrence on the themes and categories. Each of the two GAO analysts then independently reviewed the answers to all open-ended questions and placed them into one or more of the categories. The analysts then compared their coding to identify any disagreements and reached agreement on all items through discussion. For the analysis of the open-ended responses on the city's ability to respond to either an RDD or IND, we developed six categories based on the number of early response activities a city stated it could provide. Specifically, we reviewed the responses looking for whether the city would be overwhelmed, the number of specific activities the city stated it would conduct, and significant challenges it would face after the attack.

To provide important context regarding current federal activities that relate to our second and third objectives on RDD and IND response planning and federal response capabilities, we traveled to Chicago to meet with federal, regional, state, and city planners who had participated in the interagency IND regional planning effort. In addition, we met with Department of Homeland Security and FEMA officials to learn how they may use insights gained from the interagency IND regional planning effort in Chicago for use in other major cities and for developing a potential nuclear and radiological annex to the draft federal interagency operational plans for the response and recovery mission areas.

To obtain additional information for our third objective on the need and availability of federal early response support, we interviewed officials involved with federal research initiatives to close gaps in response capabilities, as well as those who oversaw planning funds and federal technical and resource assistance activities for RDD and IND attacks. Specifically, we interviewed FEMA emergency management interagency working groups, response planning, and grants officials; National Nuclear Security Administration emergency management response operations officials; Department of Energy national laboratory officials; and subject matter experts. We also reviewed relevant federal guidance documents.

We conducted this performance audit from June 2012 to September 2013 in accordance with generally accepted government auditing standards. Those standards require that we plan and perform the audit to obtain sufficient, appropriate evidence to provide a reasonable basis for our findings and conclusions based on our audit objectives. We believe that the evidence obtained provides a reasonable basis for our findings and conclusions based on our audit objectives.

APPENDIX II: QUESTIONNAIRE

 **G A O**
Accountability • Integrity • Reliability
U. S. Government Accountability Office

Survey on City Early Response to Radiological Dispersal or Improvised Nuclear Device Attack

Survey Purpose: To gather the perspectives of local emergency managers about the threat posed by a terrorist detonation of a radiological dispersal device (RDD) or improvised nuclear device (IND) and their city's capability to respond to either incident. The responses will inform Congress as it explores ways to enhance local preparedness.

The U.S. Government Accountability Office (GAO) -- a non-partisan agency of the Congress that conducts objective, fact-based research -- has been asked by the Senate Committee on Homeland Security and Governmental Affairs to study the perceived roles, responsibilities, and capabilities of major cities for early response to a terrorist attack using an RDD or IND. Either type of attack would require an effective response within the first 24 hours to characterize the dispersal of the radioactive material, communicate life-saving advice to affected populations, and to mobilize other response capabilities.

This survey will gather the perspectives of emergency managers representing the most populated city within each of the 31 Urban Areas Security Initiative (UASI) jurisdictions about the threat posed by the detonation of an RDD or IND and their capabilities in conducting **response activities during the first 24 hours after detonation**.

We need your help to provide Congress with this important information and your responses may help improve federal support to cities in the future. Your answers will be aggregated with those from all other cities and will be summarized in a report to Congress that will be publicly available. We will not publish survey responses that identify cities in our report.

We will send you a copy or a link to the report when our report is published in 2013.

This survey is not being conducted for FEMA and it is independent of any FEMA surveys or other assessments.

You were identified as the emergency management point of contact for your city. You may not have the answer to every question readily available, so please consult records or ask other people in your emergency management office for information that will allow you to answer every question. We are interested in your city-wide perspective as an emergency manager rather than the perspectives of all city departments.

Please complete and return this Microsoft Word file as an email attachment by Friday, January 4, 2013.

This questionnaire includes approximately 25 questions. Almost all questions are "Yes/No" or "checkbox" questions that can be answered very quickly.

When you are finished with this questionnaire, please save it and email it as an attachment to Eli Lewine at LewineE@gao.gov. If you have any questions, please contact Eli Lewine at LewineE@gao.gov or 202-512-3494.

Instructions

To navigate through this questionnaire, please use the tab key, up and down arrow keys, page up and page down keys, or the scroll bar. To select an answer using a check box (☐), simply use the mouse to click in the box. To remove a mark from a check box, simply click in the check box again and the "X" should disappear. To select an answer using a "drop-down" box (Example), click on the box and select a response from the list provided. To answer a question that requires that you type a comment, please click on the answer box and begin typing. The comment area will expand as you type.

Please save the file frequently to avoid losing your answers. Thank you.

1. **If a radiological dispersal device (RDD) or an improvised nuclear device (IND) detonated in your city, which of the following documents, if any, would you consult to know your city's roles and responsibilities for responding? This includes but is <u>not limited to</u> your city's response during the first 24 hours. Please select "yes" if the document's roles and responsibilities <u>apply to</u> an RDD or IND attack even if the document does not explicitly refer to an RDD or IND attack.** *Please click in the Drop-Down box to select "Yes", "No", "Not applicable", or "Don't know" for each row.*

   City emergency operations plan... SELECT ONE

   City hazard management plan .... SELECT ONE

   City continuity of operations plan .... SELECT ONE

   Regional catastrophic incident coordination plan................ SELECT ONE

   State emergency operations plan .... SELECT ONE

   State radiological emergency response plan .... SELECT ONE

   Other plans, annexes, or documents not mentioned above
   (Please describe below)... SELECT ONE

2. **What is the current state of development of your city's <u>city-wide</u> planning specifically for response to the detonation of an <u>RDD</u> in your city? This includes but is <u>not limited to</u> your city's response during the first 24 hours. This question refers to <u>city-wide</u> plans, not the plans of specific departments (e.g., police or fire department-specific plans).** *Please check only one box below.*

   Not applicable - This city is not responsible for planning
   specifically for an RDD attack... ☐

   No city-wide RDD-specific plans have been completed
   nor are any in development .... ☐   } *Skip to Question 5*

   No city-wide RDD-specific plans have been completed
   but some are in development .... ☐

   Some but not all city-wide RDD-specific plans have
   been completed .... ☐   } *Continue with "3" below*

   All city-wide RDD-specific plans that were in
   development have been completed...................................... ☐

3. If some or all city-wide <u>RDD-specific plans</u> for response to the detonation of an <u>RDD</u> have been completed, are the roles and responsibilities for your city in those plans significantly different from the local government roles and responsibilities described in the *National Response Framework* (NRF) and its supporting annexes? (<u>Control-click here</u> or direct your browser to http://www.fema.gov/pdf/emergency/nrf/nrf-core.pdf to download the National Response Framework, if desired.) *Please check only one box below.*

City's roles and responsibilities are <u>significantly different</u> from those for local governments in the NRF .... ☐ ➡ *Continue with "3a" below*

City's roles and responsibilities are <u>not</u> significantly different from those for local governments in the NRF ...... ☐

Don't know .... ☐   } *Skip to Question 4*

     3a. **If your city's roles and responsibilities are significantly different from those described for local governments in the *National Response Framework*, what are the differences?** *The box will expand as you type.*

     [   ] .

4. If some or all city-wide <u>RDD-specific plans</u> for response to the detonation of an <u>RDD</u> have been completed, has your city or will your city have participated in any exercises <u>to test the validity</u> of any of the plans between January 1, 2010 and December 31, 2012? This includes local, regional, state or federal exercises. Exercises may include workshops, facilitated policy discussions, seminars, tabletop exercises, games, modeling and simulation, drills, functional exercises, and full-scale exercises. *Please check only one box below.*

     Yes .... ☐ ➡ *Continue with "4a" below*
     No .... ☐
     Don't know ☐   } *Skip to Question 6*

     4a. **If "yes", what types of exercises were they?** Exercises may include workshops, facilitated policy discussions, seminars, tabletop exercises, games, modeling and simulation, drills, functional exercises, and full-scale exercises. *The box will expand as you type.*

     [   ]

     4b. **Were the response activities performed by the federal government -- other than those of federal law enforcement agencies -- incorporated in the execution of any of these exercises?** *Please check only one box below.*

         Yes .... ☐
         No .... ☐
         Don't know ☐

5. In Question 2 you indicated that your city does not have <u>city-wide RDD-specific</u> plans. What <u>city-wide</u> plans does your city have that <u>would apply to</u> the detonation of an RDD in your city? This question refers to <u>city-wide</u> plans, not the plans of specific departments (e.g., police or fire department-specific plans). *The box will expand as you type.*

     [   ] .

6. What is the current state of development of your city's city-wide planning specifically for response to the detonation of an IND in your city? This includes but is not limited to your city's response during the first 24 hours. This question refers to city-wide plans, not the plans of specific departments (e.g., police or fire department-specific plans). *Please check only one box below.*

Not applicable - This city is not responsible for planning specifically for an IND attack .... ☐

No city-wide IND-specific plans have been completed nor are any in development .... ☐ — *Skip to Question 9*

No city-wide IND-specific plans have been completed but some are in development .... ☐

Some but not all city-wide IND-specific plans have been completed .... ☐ — *Continue with "7" below*

All city-wide IND-specific plans that were in development have been completed................................... ☐

7. If some or all city-wide IND-specific plans for response to the detonation of an IND have been completed, are the roles and responsibilities for your city in those plans significantly different from the local government roles and responsibilities described in the *National Response Framework* (NRF) and its supporting annexes? (Control-click here or direct your browser to http://www.fema.gov/pdf/emergency/nrf/nrf-core.pdf to download the National Response Framework, if desired.) *Please check only one box below.*

City's roles and responsibilities are significantly different from those for local governments in the NRF .... ☐ → *Continue with "7a" below*

City's roles and responsibilities are not significantly different from those for local governments in the NRF ...... ☐

Don't know .... ☐ — *Skip to Question 8*

    7a. If your city's roles and responsibilities are significantly different from those described for local governments in the *National Response Framework*, what are the differences? *The box will expand as you type.*

.

8. If some or all city-wide IND-specific plans for response to the detonation of an IND have been completed, has your city or will your city have participated in any exercises to test the validity of any of the plans between January 1, 2010 and December 31, 2012? This includes local, regional, state or federal exercises. Exercises may include workshops, facilitated policy discussions, seminars, tabletop exercises, games, modeling and simulation, drills, functional exercises, and full-scale exercises. *Please check only one box below.*

Yes .... ☐ → *Continue with "8a" below*

No.............. ☐

Don't know ☐ — *Skip to Question 10*

    8a. If "yes", what types of exercises were they? Exercises may include workshops, facilitated policy discussions, seminars, tabletop exercises, games, modeling and simulation, drills, functional exercises, and full-scale exercises. *The box will expand as you type.*

8b. Were the response activities performed by the federal government -- other than those of federal law enforcement agencies -- incorporated in the execution of any of these exercises? *Please check only one box below.*

Yes .... ☐
No .... ☐
Don't know ☐

9. In Question 6 you indicated that your city does not have <u>city-wide IND-specific</u> plans. What <u>city-wide</u> plans does your city have that <u>would apply to</u> the detonation of an IND in your city? This question refers to <u>city-wide</u> plans, not the plans of specific departments (e.g., police or fire department-specific plans). *The box will expand as you type.*

```
[                                                                    ]
```
.

10. Did your city assess the risk <u>specifically of an RDD or IND</u> attack as part of your city's most-recently <u>completed</u> Hazard Identification and Vulnerability Assessment (HIVA) or similar assessment? For this survey, risk includes threat, vulnerability, and consequence. *Please check only one box below.*

Not applicable - Our city has not completed a HIVA or
   similar assessment .... ☐ ⎫ *Skip to the "Important" note before*
No, <u>neither</u> RDD nor IND threats were assessed .... ☐ ⎭ *Question 11*

Yes, but <u>only the RDD threat</u> was assessed .... ☐ → *Continue with "10b" below*

Yes, but <u>only the IND threat</u> was assessed .... ☐ → *Skip to "10c"*

Yes, both RDD and IND threats were assessed
   together as a single, <u>combined "RDD/IND" threat</u> ☐ → *Skip to "10d"*

Yes, both RDD and IND threats were assessed as
   <u>two separate threats</u> .... ☐ → *Continue with "10a" below*

    10a. If the risk of an RDD attack was assessed separately from the risk of an IND attack, how did the risk of an RDD attack rank relative to the risk of an IND attack? *Please check only one box below.*

      An RDD attack was <u>higher</u> risk than an IND attack .... ☐

      An RDD attack was approximately the <u>same</u> risk as an IND attack ☐

      An RDD attack was <u>lower</u> risk than an IND attack .... ☐

    10b. How did the risk of an <u>RDD</u> attack rank relative to all other threats and hazards? *Please check only one box below.*

      An RDD attack was <u>higher</u> risk than <u>all</u> other threats/hazards .... ☐

      An RDD attack was <u>higher</u> risk than <u>most</u> other threats/hazards .... ☐

      An RDD attack was approximately the <u>same</u> risk as <u>most</u> other threats/hazards ☐

      An RDD attack was <u>lower</u> risk than <u>most</u> other threats/hazards .... ☐

      An RDD attack was <u>lower</u> risk than <u>all</u> other threats/hazards .... ☐

10c. How did the risk of an <u>IND</u> attack rank relative to all other threats and hazards?
Please check only one box below.

Not applicable - An IND attack was not assessed..................... ☐

An IND attack was <u>higher</u> risk than <u>all</u> other threats/hazards... ☐

An IND attack was <u>higher</u> risk than <u>most</u> other threats/hazards ☐

An IND attack was approximately the <u>same</u> risk as <u>most</u> other
    threats/hazards .... ☐

An IND attack was <u>lower</u> risk than <u>most</u> other threats/hazards ☐

An IND attack was <u>lower</u> risk than <u>all</u> other threats/hazards .... ☐

Skip to the "Important" note before Question 11

10d. If the risk of an RDD or IND attack was assessed together as a single "RDD/IND" threat, how did the risk of an <u>RDD/IND</u> attack rank relative to all other threats and hazards? If they were not assessed together as a single threat, please skip to Question 8. *Please check only one box below.*

An RDD/IND attack was <u>higher</u> risk than <u>all</u> other threats/hazards .... ☐

An RDD/IND attack was <u>higher</u> risk than <u>most</u> other threats/hazards .... ☐

An RDD/IND attack was approximately the <u>same</u> risk as most other threats/hazards ☐

An RDD/IND attack was <u>lower</u> risk than <u>most</u> other threats/hazards .... ☐

An RDD/IND attack was <u>lower</u> risk than <u>all</u> other threats/hazards .... ☐

<u>IMPORTANT:</u> **There are many possible scenarios for an RDD or IND attack. It is impossible for us to ask about your city's ability to respond for all scenarios. For this survey, we will ask you some questions based on one RDD scenario and one IND scenario drawn directly from the Department of Homeland Security's National Planning Scenarios.**

<u>NOTE:</u> **The next questions apply to the following <u>RDD</u> scenario:**

Casualties	180 fatalities; 270 injuries; 20,000 detectible contaminations
Infrastructure Damage	Near the explosion
Evacuations/Displaced Persons	• 10,000 evacuated to shelters in safe areas (decontamination required prior to entering shelters) • 25,000 are given shelter-in-place instructions • Hundreds of thousands self-evacuate from major urban areas in anticipation of future attacks
Contamination	36 city blocks
Economic Impact	Up to billions of dollars
Potential for Multiple Events	Yes
Recovery Timeline	Months to years

11. In your opinion <u>as an emergency manager</u>, how able is your city to conduct the response <u>during the first 24 hours after the detonation of an RDD</u>, including mutual aid from any jurisdiction <u>other than the federal government</u>, for the scenario above? *The box will expand as you type.*

12. In your opinion <u>as an emergency manager</u>, if federal funding to your city decreased from its current level, could your city maintain its current overall ability to conduct the response <u>during the first 24 hours after the detonation of an RDD</u> for the scenario above, including mutual aid from any jurisdiction <u>other than the federal government</u>? *Please check only one box below.*

Yes, <u>could</u> sustain current overall ability .... ☐ → *Skip to Question 13*

No, could <u>not</u> sustain current overall ability ..... ☐

Don't know .... ☐ } *Continue with "12a" below*

    12a. If "no" or "don't know", please explain why below. *The box will expand as you type.*

13. Does your city have <u>city-wide plans to improve its overall ability</u> to conduct response <u>during the first 24 hours after the detonation of an RDD</u> for the scenario above, including mutual aid from any jurisdiction <u>other than the federal government</u>, beyond your city's current overall level of ability between now and December 31, <u>2013</u>? This question refers to <u>city-wide</u> plans, not the plans of specific departments (e.g., police or fire department-specific plans). *Please check only one box below.*

Yes .... ☐

No .... ☐

Don't know ☐

14. For the scenario above, do you expect the federal government to perform any response activities <u>during the first 24 hours after the detonation of an RDD</u> that neither your city, state, nor any other jurisdiction would perform? *Please check only one box below.*

Yes .... ☐ → *Continue with "14a" below*

No .... ☐

Don't know ☐ } *Skip to Question 15*

    14a. If "yes", what activities do you expect the federal government would perform <u>during the first 24 hours after the detonation of an RDD</u> for the scenario above that neither your city, state, nor any other jurisdiction would perform? *The box will expand as you type.*

15. The 2011 *National Preparedness Goal* uses an "all-hazards" approach to describe activities that may be needed to respond to all hazards and threats rather than specific hazards or threats. For the <u>RDD</u> scenario provided above, how adequate, if at all, is an "all hazards" approach for the response <u>during the first 24 hours after the detonation of an RDD</u>? (<u>Control-click here</u> or direct your browser to http://www.fema.gov/pdf/prepared/npg.pdf to download the National Preparedness Goal, if desired.) *Please check only one box below.*

Completely adequate...... ☐ ⎫
                        ⎬ *Skip to the "Note" on the next page*
Mostly adequate .... ☐ ⎭

Moderately adequate...... ☐ ⎫
Slightly adequate .... ☐ ⎬ *Continue to "15a"*
Not at all adequate .... ☐ ⎭

Don't know or no opinion ☐ ➔ *Skip to the "Note" on the next page*

> 15a. If you checked "not at all", "slightly", or "moderately adequate", what is <u>not</u> adequate about the "all-hazards" approach regarding response during the first 24 hours after the detonation of an <u>RDD</u> in your city for the RDD scenario above? *The box will expand as you type.*
>
> [ ]

NOTE: The next questions apply to the following <u>IND</u> scenario:

Casualties	Hundreds of thousands
Infrastructure Damage	Total within radius of 0.5 to 3 miles
Evacuations/Displaced Persons	• 100,000 in affected area seek shelter in safe areas (decontamination required for all before entering shelters) • 250,000 instructed to shelter in place as plume moves across region(s) • 1 million+ self-evacuate from major urban areas
Contamination	Various levels up to approximately 3,000 square miles
Economic Impact	Hundreds of billions of dollars
Potential for Multiple Events	No
Recovery Timeline	Years

16. In your opinion <u>as an emergency manager</u>, how able is your city to conduct the response <u>during the first 24 hours after the detonation of an IND</u>, including mutual aid from any jurisdiction <u>other than the federal government</u>, for the scenario above? *The box will expand as you type.*

[ ]

17. In your opinion <u>as an emergency manager</u>, if federal funding to your city decreased from its current level, could your city maintain its current overall ability to conduct the response <u>during the first 24 hours after the detonation of an IND</u> for the scenario above, including mutual aid from any jurisdiction <u>other than the federal government</u>? *Please check only one box below.*

Yes, <u>could</u> sustain current overall ability .... ☐ ➔ *Skip to Question 18*
No, could <u>not</u> sustain current overall ability..... ☐ ⎫
                                         ⎬ *Continue with "17a" below*
Don't know .... ☐ ⎭

17a. If "no" or "don't know", please explain why below. *The box will expand as you type.*

[ ]

18. Does your city have <u>city-wide plans to improve its overall ability</u> to conduct response <u>during the first 24 hours after the detonation of an IND</u> for the scenario above, including mutual aid from any jurisdiction <u>other than the federal government</u>, beyond your city's current overall level of ability between now and December 31, 2013? This question refers to <u>city-wide</u> plans, not the plans of specific departments (e.g., police or fire department-specific plans). *Please check only one box below.*

Yes............ [ ]
No.............. [ ]
Don't know [ ]

19. For the scenario above, do you expect the federal government to perform any response activities <u>during the first 24 hours after the detonation of an IND</u> that neither your city, state, nor any other jurisdiction would perform? *Please check only one box below.*

Yes............ [ ] → *Continue with "19a" below*
No.............. [ ]
Don't know [ ] *Skip to Question 20*

    19a. If "yes", what activities do you expect the federal government would perform <u>during the first 24 hours after the detonation of an IND</u> for the scenario above that neither your city, state, nor any other jurisdiction would perform? *The box will expand as you type.*

[ ]

20. The 2011 *National Preparedness Goal* uses an "all-hazards" approach to describe activities that may be needed to respond to all hazards and threats rather than specific hazards or threats. For the <u>IND</u> scenario provided above, how adequate, if at all, is an "all hazards" approach for the response <u>during the first 24 hours after the detonation of an IND</u>? (<u>Control-click here</u> or direct your browser to http://www.fema.gov/pdf/prepared/npg.pdf to download the National Preparedness Goal, if desired.) *Please check only one box below.*

Completely adequate...... [ ]
Mostly adequate .... [ ] *Skip to Question 21*

Moderately adequate...... [ ]
Slightly adequate........... [ ] *Continue to "20a"*
Not at all adequate .... [ ]

Don't know or no opinion [ ] → *Skip to Question 21*

    20a. If you checked "not at all", "slightly", or "moderately adequate", what is <u>not</u> adequate about the "all-hazards" approach regarding response during the first 24 hours after the detonation of an <u>IND</u> in your city for the IND scenario above? *The box will expand as you type.*

[ ]

Final Questions:

21. The federal government may support research that could improve procedures or information that could be used during the first 24 hours after the detonation of an RDD or IND, but needs to focus its resources on those areas that would provide the greatest impact. In your opinion as an emergency manager, how much impact, if any, would improving procedures or information in each of the following topic areas have on your city's ability to respond during the first 24 hours after the detonation of an RDD or IND? This question applies to any RDD or IND scenario and is not limited to the specific scenarios presented earlier. *Please click in the Drop-Down box to select "No impact", "Very low impact", "Low impact", "Moderate impact", "High impact", "Very high impact", or "Don't know/No opinion" for each area.*

Improving procedures or information related to modeling the predicted dispersal of radioactive materials .... SELECT ONE

Improving procedures or information related to measuring the actual, real-time dispersal of radioactive materials .... SELECT ONE

Improving procedures or information related to predicting impacts on the city's physical infrastructure .... SELECT ONE

Improving procedures or information related to predicting radiological impacts on people .... SELECT ONE

Improving procedures or information related to communicating potential impacts of radiation exposure to the public .... SELECT ONE

Improving procedures or information related to early decontamination of people .... SELECT ONE

Improving procedures or information related to early decontamination of buildings.. SELECT ONE

Improving procedures or information related to mass evacuation .... SELECT ONE

Improving procedures or information related to communicating a sheltering-in-place strategy to the public... SELECT ONE

Improving procedures or information related to developing a strategy for relocating the public to emergency shelters................................... SELECT ONE

21a. If there are other topic areas in which improving procedures or information would have a "High" or "Very high" impact on your city's ability to respond during the first 24 hours after the detonation of an RDD or IND, please type them in the box below. *The box will expand as you type.*

22. In 2012, did or will your city follow the Threat and Hazard Identification and Risk Assessment (THIRA) approach, described in the 2012 THIRA Comprehensive Preparedness Guide 201, to identify your city's threats and hazards and assess associated risks and impacts? (Control-click here or direct your browser to http://www.fema.gov/library/file?type=publishedFile&file=cpg_201_thira_guide_final_040312.pdf&fileid=b8f77f90-7e65-11e1-8178-001cc456982e to download Comprehensive Preparedness Guide 201, if desired.) *Please check only one box below.*

Yes .... ☐ → *Continue with "22a" below*

No.............. ☐
‾‾‾‾‾‾‾‾‾‾‾‾‾‾‾‾‾ } *Skip to Question 23*
Don't know ☐

22a. If "yes", did or will your city's THIRA <u>explicitly</u> include the threat of an RDD attack or an IND attack or both? *Please check only one box below.*

No, <u>neither</u> RDD nor IND threats were explicitly included . ☐ ⎫

Yes, but <u>only the RDD threat</u> was explicitly included .... ☐ ⎬ *Continue with*

Yes, but <u>only the IND threat</u> was explicitly included .... ☐ ⎭ *"22a1" below*

Yes, both RDD and IND threats were explicitly included
together as a single, <u>combined "RDD/IND" threat</u>..... ☐ ⎫

Yes, both RDD and IND threats were explicitly included   ⎬ *Skip to Question 23*
as <u>two separate threats</u> .... ☐ ⎭

    22a1. If "no", "yes but only RDD", or "yes but only IND", why was an RDD or IND threat or both threats not explicitly included in your city's THIRA? *The box will expand as you type.*

    [   ]

23. Has your city participated in preparing your Urban Area Security Initiative's (UASI) 2012 THIRA? *Please check only one box below.*

Yes .... ☐

No .... ☐

Don't know ☐

24. The results of this survey will be provided in a report to Congress. If you could tell Congress the most-important ways that the federal government could improve cities' responses to an RDD or IND attack what would those ways be? This includes but is <u>not limited to</u> a city's response during the first 24 hours. *The box will expand as you type.*

[   ] .

25. In case we have follow-up questions about the answers in this questionnaire, please provide the following information about the person we should contact:

Point of contact (POC) name:	
POC's title:	
POC's organization:	
POC's phone number:	
POC's email address:	

Please save this questionnaire and return it to Eli Lewine at LewineE@gao.gov.

Thank you very much.

APPENDIX III: FISCAL YEAR 2013 DHS PREPAREDNESS GRANT PROGRAMS FUNDING AWARDED

Preparedness grant programs	Grant programs purpose	FY 2013 funding awarded
Homeland Security Grant Program (HSGP) Comprised of three related grant programs: State Homeland Security Program (SHSP), Urban Areas Security Initiative (UASI), and Operation Stonegarden (OPSG).	For states and urban areas to prevent, protect against, mitigate, respond to, and recover from acts of terrorism and other threats.	Over $968 million (HSGP) Over $354 million (SHSP) Over $558 million (UASI) $55 million (OPSG) Over $968 million (HSGP)
• State Homeland Security Program	To support the implementation of state homeland security strategies to build and strengthen preparedness capabilities at all levels.	Over $354 million
• Urban Areas Security Initiative	To enhance regional preparedness and capabilities in 31 high-threat, high-density areas.	Over $558 million
• Operation Stonegarden	To enhance cooperation and coordination among federal, state, territorial, tribal and local law enforcement agencies to jointly enhance security along the United States land and water borders.	$55 million
Emergency Management Performance Grants Program	To assist state and local governments in enhancing and sustaining all hazards emergency management capabilities.	Over $332 million

Preparedness grant programs	Grant programs purpose	FY 2013 funding awarded
Tribal Homeland Security Grant Program	To implement preparedness initiatives to help strengthen the nation against risk associated with hazards including terrorist attacks.	$10 million
Nonprofit Security Grant Program	To support physical security enhancements for nonprofit organizations determined to be at high risk of a terrorist attack and located within one of the FY 2012 UASI-eligible urban areas.	$10 million
Intercity Passenger Rail (Amtrak) Program	To protect critical surface transportation infrastructure and the traveling public from terrorism and increase Amtrak rail system resilience.	Over $9 million
Port Security Grant Program	To protect critical port infrastructure from terrorism, enhance maritime domain awareness, and strengthen risk management capabilities to protect against improvised explosive devices and other nonconventional weapons.	Over $93 million
Transit Security Grant Program	To protect critical surface transportation and the traveling public from acts of terrorism and to increase the resilience of transit infrastructure.	Over $83 million
Total Awarded		**Over $1.5 billion**

Source: DHS.

End Notes

[1] RDDs and INDs are considered weapons of mass destruction, along with chemical and biological weapons. See 18 U.S.C. § 2332a(c); 6 U.S.C. § 485(a)(6).

[2] Fissile material is composed of atoms that can be split by neutrons in a self-sustaining chain reaction to release enormous amounts of energy. In nuclear weapons, the fission energy is released all at once to produce a violent explosion. The primary fissile materials are plutonium and uranium.

[3] The term "response," refers to those capabilities necessary to save lives, protect property and the environment, and meet basic human needs after an incident has occurred.

[4] National Science and Technology Council, *Nuclear Defense Research and Development Roadmap, Fiscal Years 2013-2017* (Washington, D.C.: Executive Office of the President, April 2012).

[5] The White House, *Presidential Policy Directive/PPD-8: National Preparedness* (Washington, D.C.: Mar. 30, 2011). DHS, *National Preparedness Report* (Washington, D.C.: Mar. 30, 2012).

[6] An incident is an occurrence or event—natural, technological, or human-caused—that requires a response to protect life, property, or the environment.

[7] DHS, *National Preparedness Goal*, First Edition (Washington, D.C.: September 2011).

[8] The FIOP is intended to provide a detailed concept of operations, description of critical tasks and responsibilities, detailed resources, personnel, and sourcing requirements, and specific provisions for the delivery of capabilities by the federal government.

[9] DHS, *National Preparedness System* (Washington, D.C.: November 2011).

[10] DHS, *National Planning Scenarios* (Washington, D.C.: March 2006). The planning scenarios include a large IND attack; biological attack-aerosol anthrax; biological disease outbreak-pandemic influenza; biological attack- plague; chemical attack-blister agent; chemical attack-toxic industrial chemicals; chemical attack- nerve agent; chemical attack- chlorine tank explosion; natural disaster-major earthquake; natural disaster-major hurricane; radiological attack-RDD; explosive attack- bombing using improvised explosive device; biological attack-food contamination; biological attack-foreign animal disease (e.g., foot-and-mouth disease); and cyber attack.

[11] DHS, *National Incident Management System* (Washington, D.C.: December 2008). This document is an update from the original 2004 publication.

[12] FEMA accomplishes this responsibility through the Federal Radiological Preparedness Coordinating Committee. The federal response mechanisms include the Emergency Support Functions and supporting annexes to the *National Response Framework,* and existing emergency response plans that address nuclear and radiological incidents.

[13] Generally, DOD resources are committed only after approval by the Secretary of Defense or at the direction of the President.

[14] The 31 major cities supported by the fiscal year 2012 Urban Areas Security Initiative program are Anaheim, Atlanta, Baltimore, Boston, Charlotte, Chicago, Dallas, Denver, Detroit, Houston, Indianapolis, Kansas City, Las Vegas, Los Angeles, Miami, Minneapolis, Newark, New Orleans, New York City, Orlando, Philadelphia, Phoenix, Portland (OR), Riverside, San Antonio, San Diego, San Francisco, Seattle, St. Louis, Tampa, and the District of Columbia. We were unable to contact emergency managers in two cities, Atlanta and Newark.

[15] Jonathan Medalia, *"Dirty Bombs": Technical Background, Attack Prevention and Response, Issues for Congress* (Washington, D.C.: Congressional Research Service, June 24, 2011).

[16] FEMA, *Regional Planning Guide* (Washington, D.C: March 2010), FEMA, *Developing and Maintaining Emergency Operations Plans: Comprehensive Preparedness Guide (CPG) 101,* Version 2.0 (Washington, D.C.: November 2010).

[17] DHS, *National Preparedness System* (Washington, D.C.: November 2011).

[18] DHS, "Planning Guidance for Protection and Recovery Following Radiological Dispersal Device (RDD) and Improvised Nuclear Device (IND) Incidents (73 Fed. Reg. 45-029 (Aug. 1, 2008); and National Security Staff Interagency Policy Coordination Subcommittee for Preparedness & Response to Radiological and Nuclear Threats, *Planning Guidance for Response to a Nuclear Detonation,* Second Edition (Washington, D.C.: June 2010).

[19] National Council on Radiation Protection and Measurements, *Responding to a Radiological or Nuclear Terrorism Incident: A Guide for Decision Makers,* Report No. 165 (Bethesda, MD: 2010); Conference on Radiation Control Program Directors, Inc., *Responding to a Radiological Dispersal Device: First Responder's Guide—The* First 12 Hours (Frankfort, KY: September 2006); and Schoch-Spane, et al., *Rad Resilient City: A Preparedness Checklist for Cities to Diminish Lives Lost From Radiation after a Nuclear Terrorist Attack* (Baltimore, MD: Center for Biosecurity of UPMC, September 2011).

[20] According to FEMA officials and some city emergency managers we spoke with, the Hazard Identification and Vulnerability Assessment is also referred to as a Hazard Identification and Risk Assessment by some cities. They stated that both titles refer to the same type of document. Many of the major cities are adopting a new process, the Threat and Hazard Identification and Risk Assessment that FEMA requires its regional offices, states, and Urban Areas Security Initiative locations to use.

[21] In accordance with the National Incidence Management System, a response plan is to address the tactics and support activities required for the planned operational period, generally the first 12 to 24 hours after the event.

[22] FEMA, *Nationwide Plan Review: Fiscal Year 2010 Report to Congress* (Washington, D.C.: July 2010). FEMA reviewed emergency operations plans for 75 major cities, which include the 27 cities that responded to our questionnaire.

[23] This question requested a self-assessment because FEMA currently uses self- assessments to gauge local response capabilities and has not yet developed performance measures to determine actual levels of capability for incident response.

[24] DHS, "Planning Guidance for Protection and Recovery Following Radiological Dispersal Device (RDD) and Improvised Nuclear Device (IND) Incidents" (73 Fed. Reg. 45-029, Aug. 1, 2008).

[25] DHS, "Nuclear/Radiological Incident Annex" to the *National Response Framework* (Washington, D.C.: June 2008). According to a FEMA official, FEMA intends to replace this 2008 annex with the nuclear and radiological annex under consideration and, because this new annex will be more of an operational guide, it will be annexed to the all hazards FIOPs for the response and recovery missions.

[26] DHS, Emergency Support Function #10—Oil and Hazardous Materials Response Annex to the *National Response Framework* (Washington, D.C.: May 2013).

[27] DHS, "Planning Guidance for Protection and Recovery Following Radiological Dispersal Device (RDD) and Improvised Nuclear Device (IND) Incidents" (73 Fed. Reg. 45-029, Aug. 1, 2008).

[28] The RDD attack depicted in the *National Planning Scenario* would contaminate 36 city blocks, causing 180 fatalities, 270 injuries, and 20,000 detectible contaminations, requiring 10,000 people to seek shelters and prompting hundreds of thousands to self-evacuate in anticipation of future attacks.

[29] The IND attack depicted in the *National Planning Scenario* would contaminate up to 3,000 square miles, causing hundreds of thousands casualties and damage up to a radius of .5 to 3 miles, requiring 100,000 people to seek shelter after being decontaminated and prompting 1 million to self-evacuate from the city.

[30] DHS, *Interim IND CONPLAN: Federal Interagency Improved Nuclear Device Concept of Operations Plan,* Version 10 (Washington, D.C.: Nov. 17, 2009).

[31] National Security Staff, DHS, *Planning Guidance for Response to a Nuclear Detonation,* Second Edition (Washington, D.C. Interagency Policy Coordinating Subcommittee for Preparedness & Response to Radiological and Nuclear Threats, June 2010).

[32] Planning guidance recommendations were provided for consideration by emergency planners within the first days after an IND attack for 1) shelter and evacuation, 2) medical care, 3) population monitoring and decontamination, and 4) emergency public information.

[33] GAO, *Managing Preparedness Grants and Assessing National Capabilities: Continuing Challenges Impede FEMA's Progress,* GAO-12-526T *(Washington, D.C.: Mar. 20, 2012).*

[34] *DHS, Response and Recovery Knowledge Product: Key Planning Factors for Recovery from a Radiological Terrorism Incident* (Washington, D.C.: September 2012).

[35] FEMA, *Developing and Maintaining Emergency Operations Plans: Comprehensive Preparedness Guide (CPG) 101, Version 2.0* (Washington, D.C.: November 2010).

[36] FEMA, *Improvised Nuclear Device Regional Operations Plan: Region V, State of Illinois, and City of Chicago Operations Plan* (Chicago, IL: June 2012).

[37] Public health and medical services provide lifesaving medical treatment and provide support and products to avoid additional disease and injury. Operational coordination establishes and maintains a unified and coordinated operational structure. On-scene security and protection ensures a safe and secure environment through law enforcement and other operations.

[38] We developed the list of current federal IND focus areas from the following two DHS reports: DHS, *DHS Strategy for Improving the National Response and Recovery from an IND Attack* (Washington, D.C.: March 24, 2010) and DHS, *Improvised Nuclear Device Response and Recovery Capability- Based Implementation Plan: Methods, Plans, and Projects for Addressing the Capability Gaps Identified in the DHS Strategy for Improving the National Response and Recovery from an IND Attack* (Washington, D.C.: March 2012), and the Executive Office of the President, National Science and Technology Council, *Nuclear Defense Research and Development Roadmap, Fiscal Years 2013- 2017* (Washington, D.C.: April 2012).

[39] The six IND focus area working groups are the Manage the Response, Crisis Decision- making, Communications and Public Messaging, Scientific Support, Public Health and Medical, and Recovery. Multiple federal agencies participate in these focus area working groups along with members from state and local emergency management offices and first responders (fire, police, emergency medical services, and public work officials). Nongovernment organizations such as medical practitioners, ethicists, clergy, biologists, sociologists, and university and private industry representatives also participate.

[40] The seven DHS grant programs are the Homeland Security Grant Program, Emergency Management Performance Grants Program, Tribal Homeland Security Grant Program, Nonprofit Security Grant Program, Intercity Passenger Rail (Amtrak) Program, Port Security Grant Program, and the Transit Security Grant Program. From fiscal years 2002 through 2011, the federal government appropriated over $37 billion to DHS's preparedness grant programs to enhance the capabilities of state and local governments to prevent, protect against, respond to, and recover from terrorist attacks.

[41] FEMA could query its Biannual Strategy Implementation Report database to determine the level of funding used for the general category of chemical, biological, radiological, nuclear, and explosives.

[42] From 2007 through 2011 the Regional Catastrophic Planning Grant Program provided more than $147 million in funding. The *Regional Catastrophic Preparedness Grant Program Comprehensive Report,* February 2012 lists 10 sites as receiving this funding including the San Francisco Bay Area, Boston, Chicago, Hampton Roads (24 jurisdictions in southeast Virginia and northeast North Carolina), Honolulu, Houston, Los Angeles, the National Capital Region, New York/New Jersey/Connecticut/Pennsylvania, and the Puget Sound region (8 Washington state counties and their associated cities).

[43] The 31 major cities in the UASI program in fiscal year 2012 were Anaheim, Atlanta, Baltimore, Boston, Charlotte, Chicago, Dallas, Denver, Detroit, Houston, Indianapolis, Kansas City, Las Vegas, Los Angeles, Miami, Minneapolis, Newark, New Orleans, New York City, Orlando, Philadelphia, Phoenix, Portland (OR), Riverside, San Antonio, San Diego, San Francisco, Seattle, St. Louis, Tampa, and the District of Columbia.

[44] The questionnaire is reproduced in full in appendix II.

[45] Three cities, Tampa, Philadelphia, and Los Angeles, did not receive e-mail notifications because they responded later than other cities to our initial contact attempts. They instead received by e-mail the cover letter and questionnaire on the same days in late December 2012 that they responded to us.

In: Nuclear Terrorism
Editor: Casey A. Lloyd

ISBN: 978-1-62948-696-3
© 2014 Nova Science Publishers, Inc.

Chapter 2

"DIRTY BOMBS": BACKGROUND IN BRIEF[*]

Jonathan Medalia

SUMMARY

Congress has long sought, through legislation and oversight, to protect the United States against terrorist threats, especially from chemical, biological, radiological, and nuclear (CBRN) weapons. Radiological dispersal devices (RDDs) are one type of CBRN weapon. Explosive-driven "dirty bombs" are an often-discussed type of RDD, though radioactive material can also be dispersed in other ways. This report provides background for understanding the RDD threat and responses, and presents issues for Congress.

Radioactive material is the necessary ingredient for an RDD. This material is composed of atoms that decay, emitting radiation. Some types and amounts of radiation are harmful to human health.

Terrorists have shown some interest in RDDs. They could use these weapons in an attempt to cause panic, area denial, and economic dislocation. While RDDs would be far less harmful than nuclear weapons, they are much simpler to build and the needed materials are used worldwide. Accordingly, some believe terrorists would be more likely to use RDDs than nuclear weapons. Key points include:

---

[*] This is an edited, reformatted and augmented version of a Congressional Research Service publication, CRS Report for Congress, R41891, dated June 24, 2011.

- RDDs could contaminate areas with radioactive material, increasing long-term cancer risks, but would probably kill few people promptly. Nuclear weapons could destroy much of a city, kill tens of thousands of people, and contaminate much larger areas with fallout.
- Cleanup cost after an RDD attack could range from less than a billion dollars to tens of billions of dollars, depending on area contaminated, decontamination technologies used, and level of cleanup required.
- Terrorists would face obstacles to using RDDs, such as obtaining materials, designing an effective weapon, and avoiding detection.

Governments and organizations have taken steps to prevent an RDD attack. Domestically, the Nuclear Regulatory Commission has issued regulations to secure radioactive sources. The Department of Homeland Security develops and operates equipment to detect radioactive material. The National Nuclear Security Administration has recovered thousands of disused or abandoned sources. Some state and local governments have taken steps to prepare for an RDD attack. Internationally, the International Atomic Energy Agency has led efforts to secure radioactive sources. Its Code of Conduct on the Safety and Security of Radioactive Sources offers guidance for protecting sources. The G8 Global Partnership has secured sources in Russia and elsewhere. Other nations have taken steps to secure sources as well. Key points include:

- Nuclear Regulatory Commission actions have done much to instill a security culture for U.S. licensees of radioactive sources post-9/11.
- Many programs have sought to improve the security of radioactive sources overseas, but some incidents raise questions about security.

Should prevention fail, federal, state, and local governments have taken many measures to respond to and recover from an RDD attack. The National Response Framework "establishes a comprehensive, national, all-hazards approach to domestic incident response." The federal government has expertise and equipment to use for recovery. Key points include:

- Government agencies have done much to prepare for and recover from an RDD attack. This work would help cope with other disasters. Conversely, planning for other disasters would help in the event of an RDD attack.

- Response planning fell short in the wake of Katrina and the Gulf oil spill, raising questions about the effectiveness of planning to respond to an RDD attack.

Issues for Congress include:

- The priority for countering RDDs vs. other types of CBRN weapons.
- The proper balance of effort for securing domestic vs. overseas radioactive sources.
- Whether to establish a radiation detection system in cities; how to dispose of potentially large volumes of radioactive waste that could result from an RDD attack.
- Whether to modify the pace of a program for implementing certain security enhancements for U.S. radioactive sources.
- How to improve radiological forensics capability.

RADIATION AND ITS EFFECTS

Radioactive materials are used worldwide for medical, industrial, research, and other purposes. Yet their security is far from airtight, especially in foreign countries. Terrorists could create a radiological dispersal device (RDD) by obtaining radioactive material and detonating an explosive next to it. An attack could contaminate some square miles, disrupt the economy, cost tens of billions of dollars to remediate, increase the long-term cancer rate, and cause panic in the target area and beyond. While the press focuses on explosive-driven "dirty bombs," terrorists could also disperse radioactive material from aircraft or in other ways. This report examines radiation and its effects, steps to prevent, respond to, and recover from an attack, and issues for Congress.

Many atoms are stable: they remain in their current form indefinitely. Some are unstable, or radioactive. They "decay," often by emitting energetic particles.[1] Gamma rays, a form of electromagnetic radiation, are often emitted by decay. Each radioactive atom, or "radionuclide," decays in a specific way. Some high-energy radiation is "ionizing." Most atoms have no net electrical charge because they have an equal number of positively-charged protons and negatively-charged electrons. Ionizing radiation knocks electrons off atoms, turning atoms into positively-charged ions that damage living cells. Very low doses of radiation produce few if any effects, but progressively higher doses may increase the risk of cancer or may cause radiation sickness or death. In the

United States, dose is usually measured in units of rem. This unit takes into account the amount of radiation absorbed and its biological effects. The average background dose for the U.S. population is estimated at 620 millirem (mrem; 1,000 mrem = 1 rem) per year.[2] About half is from natural sources, and half from exposure for medical purposes.

An RDD attack is likely to expose few people to a dose of more than a few rem per year. Views differ on the harm from that dose. One view is that any amount of radiation increases cancer risk; another is that there is no evidence that radiation of less than about 10 rem per year increases that risk. Federal standards differ for low doses. For dose to the public resulting from the nuclear fuel cycle (e.g., nuclear power plants), the Environmental Protection Agency (EPA) uses a standard of 25 mrem per year of whole-body dose.[3] In contrast, the Nuclear Regulatory Commission (NRC) has established an occupational dose limit of 5 rem per year.[4] No single level marks the line between an acceptable and unacceptable dose.

An RDD attack would elevate dose in the affected area beyond the background dose. The EPA issued guidance for protective actions following nuclear and radiological incidents except nuclear war, and the Federal Emergency Management Agency (FEMA) issued guidance for actions following RDD and improvised nuclear device (IND, i.e., a terrorist-made nuclear weapon) incidents.[5] Both agencies recommended "protective action guides" (PAGs). A PAG is "the projected dose to a reference individual, from an accidental or deliberate release of radioactive material, at which a specific protective action to reduce or avoid that dose is recommended."[6]

FEMA divides incident response into phases. For the early phase, which starts "at the beginning of the incident,"[7] the protective action recommended for a PAG of 1 to 5 rem is sheltering in place or evacuation. The intermediate phase "is usually assumed to begin after the incident source and releases have been brought under control." For it, FEMA recommends "relocation of the public" for a projected dose of 2 rem for the first year and 0.5 rem per year for any subsequent year. The late phase starts when recovery and cleanup begin, and ends with their completion. FEMA does not have a PAG for the late phase because authorities would need to optimize among economic, land use, etc., in determining which areas need to be remediated to what levels.

As a guide to quantities of material that should be protected, in 2003 the International Atomic Energy Agency (IAEA) revised its Code of Conduct on the Safety and Security of Radioactive Sources.[8] The IAEA decided that the code "should serve as guidance to States for—*inter alia*— the development and harmonization of policies, laws and regulations on the safety and security of radioactive sources."[9] It lists 16 radionuclides that are in common use and could pose a threat. For each radionuclide, the code lists three categories of radiation and the threshold radiation value for each category based on potential to harm individuals. Category 1 sources are those that, if not safely managed or securely protected, could cause permanent injury to someone who handled them for a few minutes, and death to someone who handled them unshielded for a few minutes to an hour. For Category 2 sources, the corresponding figures are minutes to hours and hours to days. Category 3 sources could cause injury to someone handling them for some hours.[10] Of the 16 radionuclides, cesium-137 chloride is of particular concern.[11] Category 2 quantities are often a fraction of a gram. Somewhat larger amounts can contaminate a substantial area. For example, **Figure 1** models a possible RDD attack on Washington, DC, using about 50 grams of cesium-137 chloride, which contaminates, to different levels, 0.81 to 5.10 square miles. The Energy Policy Act of 2005 (P.L. 109-58) mandates certain security measures for Category 1 and 2 sources. The NRC considers Category 2 sources to be risk-significant.[12] Since the NRC judges that Category 2 sources could cause significant economic effects, it uses Category 2 as the basis for mandating security measures beyond those in the Energy Policy Act.

THREATS AND IMPEDIMENTS

An RDD could cause prompt casualties, which would most likely come only from the explosion of a dirty bomb; panic; economic disruption, which might result if a port or city center were contaminated with radioactive material; asset denial, in which public concern over the presence of radioactive material might lead people to abandon a subway system or an area of a city for months to years; a requirement for decontamination, which would be costly; and long-term casualties resulting from exposure to or inhalation of radioactive material. A study of the economic impacts of an attack on the ports of Los Angeles and Long Beach using two RDDs placed total U.S. losses at $8.5 billion for exports and $26.0 billion for imports.[13]

While there have been thefts of radioactive material and attempts to use it for malevolent ends,[14] there has not been a successful RDD attack, for reasons such as the following. Terrorists would need to learn about radiation for self-protection. They would need to learn which radioactive materials would be suitable for an RDD. They would have to obtain the material despite security measures. They would have to move the material past detectors at U.S. ports and elsewhere. They would have to acquire the other bomb components, assemble the bomb, and place it, steps that law enforcement might detect. Forensic analysis might reveal the perpetrator of the attack, possibly leading to retaliation and deterring state assistance. While no one reason presents an insurmountable obstacle, the combination may help explain why an RDD attack has not occurred.

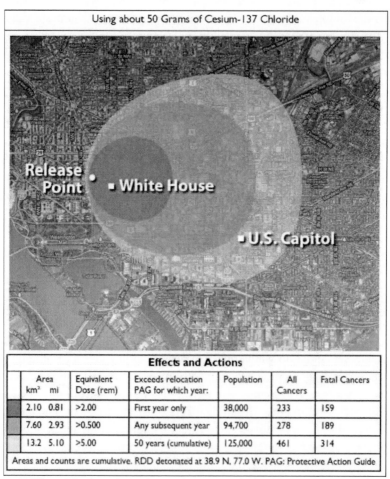

Using about 50 Grams of Cesium-137 Chloride

Effects and Actions

Area km² mi	Equivalent Dose (rem)	Exceeds relocation PAG for which year:	Population	All Cancers	Fatal Cancers
2.10 0.81	>2.00	First year only	38,000	233	159
7.60 2.93	>0.500	Any subsequent year	94,700	278	189
13.2 5.10	>5.00	50 years (cumulative)	125,000	461	314

Areas and counts are cumulative. RDD detonated at 38.9 N, 77.0 W. PAG: Protective Action Guide

Source: William Rhodes III, Senior Manager, International Security Systems Group, Sandia National Laboratories, September 2010; analysis by Heather Pennington; graphics by Mona Aragon.

Notes: (provided by William Rhodes): This map, based on an atmospheric dispersion model, shows where individuals are projected to have an increased risk of developing cancers due to radiation exposure over a year or more. The RDD in this scenario uses about 50 grams of cesium-137 chloride. The model assumes that all material used is dispersed, but that it is not dispersed evenly over the area. Wind is assumed to be from west to east at 7 mph. The model includes exposure from radioactive material both deposited on the surface and resuspended into the air and inhaled. EPA and FEMA have developed Protective Action Guides (PAGs) to indicate when long-term relocation of individuals should be considered. PAGs are primarily based on an assessment of the increased risk of developing cancer over an exposed individual's lifetime. They assume, conservatively, that individuals are unsheltered and remain in the area during the entire period described for each contour. Contours show where individuals, if not relocated per the PAG, are projected to receive at least a specified dose in a specified time, as follows: inner contour (red), dose in first year post-attack, >2.00 rem; middle contour (orange), dose in second year post-attack, >0.500 rem; and outer contour (yellow), cumulative dose in the first 50 years post-attack. >5.00 rem. The cigar-shaped plumes often seen in models of atmospheric dispersion occur for gases or very fine particles, which would be the case for chemical warfare agents or fallout from a nuclear weapon but not in the case depicted. Whether such plumes would occur for an RDD depends on such factors as wind speed, type of explosive, and particle size.

Figure 1. A Possible RDD Attack on Washington, DC.

PREVENTING AN ATTACK: DOMESTIC EFFORTS

Before September 11, 2001, the main concern for radioactive sources was their safe handling. They were used worldwide in many applications with varying levels of security. The ongoing U.S. response to the attacks is based on "layered defense," in which each layer increases the likelihood of disrupting a possible attack. Layers includes protecting sources through licensing, tracking, and physical security upgrades; removing sources that are outside the tracking system because they are abandoned, lost, or stolen; and reducing the number of sources in use.

Securing Radioactive Sources

Since materials of greatest concern for use in an RDD are made in nuclear reactors, terrorists could only obtain them through transfer from sympathetic insiders, theft, or purchase. Securing radioactive sources therefore reduces the risk of an RDD attack. Many government agencies and other entities have taken steps to secure these sources.

The Nuclear Regulatory Commission (NRC), an independent agency, "has the responsibility to license and regulate the civilian use of radioactive materials for commercial, industrial, academic, and medical purposes in a manner that protects public health and safety and promotes the common defense and security. The NRC and its predecessor, the Atomic Energy Commission (AEC), have regulated the use of radioactive materials since 1946."[15] Since 9/11, the NRC has issued orders and regulations requiring its licensees to take various measures to enhance radiation source security.

The National Nuclear Security Administration (NNSA) is a semiautonomous agency within the Department of Energy. The Global Threat Reduction Initiative (GTRI) is a key NNSA program to enhance the security of radioactive sources. GTRI's Domestic Materials Protection Program enhances security for domestic radioactive sources on a voluntary basis, and pays for upgrades and initial maintenance. GTRI's Off-site Source Recovery Project recovers sources in the United States and abroad that have been lost, abandoned, or stolen, or are excess to a user's needs. As of March 28, 2011, OSRP had recovered 24,029 sources in the United States.[16]

The Energy Policy Act of 2005 established the **Radiation Source Protection and Security Task Force** with a mandate to "evaluate, and provide recommendations relating to, the security of radiation sources in the United States from potential terrorist threats." Its members represent many federal agencies. Its 2010 report[17] identified two major challenges, access to disposal pathways for unused sources, and alternatives to several risk-significant radioactive sources.

The Environmental Protection Agency (EPA) "is seeking to reduce the number of sealed radiation sources used in industrial devices and applications. Through its Alternative Technologies Initiative, the Agency has been working with industry since 2001 to identify non- nuclear substitutes."[18] The Domestic Nuclear Detection Office, a component of the Department of Homeland Security (DHS), is supporting similar R&D through its Small Business Innovative Research program. The Department of Defense (DOD) has some sealed sources in the United States, such as at hospitals. The NRC grants DOD components one or more licenses, and they protect the sources in accordance with NRC regulations.[19]

How Secure Are Radioactive Sources in the United States?

NRC notes such security violations as "inoperable or ineffective physical protection systems" and "incomplete or inadequate plan with local law enforcement."[20] The Radiation Source Protection and Security Task Force stated, "Every year, thousands of sources become disused and unwanted in the United States. ... the longer sources remain disused or unwanted the chances increase that they will become unsecured or abandoned."[21] (Most of these sources have a very low level of radioactivity and do not pose a significant risk.[22]) Nonetheless, there have been "no successful thefts or sabotage" of higher-level sources,[23] and there has never been a successful RDD attack. NRC data show that from the third quarter of FY2006 through the second quarter of FY2010, no Category 1 or 2 sources were lost, and 17 Category 3 sources were lost but all were recovered.[24]

Detecting Radioactive Sources

U.S. Customs and Border Protection, a DHS component, has deployed systems at ports and border crossings to detect and identify radioactive material (and other contraband) entering the United States. Other DHS components deploy radiation detection equipment at other sites inside the United States, and the Domestic Nuclear Detection Office has a cooperative program with state and local agencies to deploy such equipment. These systems seek to detect terrorist nuclear weapons or nuclear-weapon material while minimizing the impact on legitimate commerce, but could detect RDD-suitable material as well.

Intelligence and Counterterrorism

Many U.S. agencies contribute and analyze intelligence on potential CBRN terrorist threats. The 9/11 Commission noted shortcomings in the Intelligence Community.[25] In response, Congress passed the Intelligence Reform and Terrorism Prevention Act of 2004 (IRTPA, P.L. 108-458). This act established the position of Director of National Intelligence, who is to "serve as head of the intelligence community." Section 6905, "Radiological Dispersal Devices," makes it unlawful to acquire or possess RDDs. IRTPA established the National Counterterrorism Center to analyze and integrate intelligence on terrorism, except that pertaining to domestic terrorists and domestic counterterrorism. IRTPA directed the President to establish the National Counter Proliferation Center to analyze proliferation-related intelligence. Within the United States, the Federal Bureau of Investigation is the lead agency for counterterrorism intelligence. It "created a Directorate of Intelligence in its headquarters to produce intelligence analysis."[26]

PREVENTING AN ATTACK: GLOBAL EFFORTS

Securing Radioactive Sources

Because an RDD attack might occur outside the United States, or material obtained abroad might be used for an RDD attack on this nation, the United States and others—including international organizations and foreign governments—are working to secure sources worldwide.

International Organizations

International Atomic Energy Agency (IAEA)

The IAEA, a U.N. organization, has responsibilities in such areas as nuclear energy, peaceful applications of nuclear science and technology, nuclear nonproliferation, and nuclear safety and security. It has the lead international role in efforts to secure radioactive sources. For example, it issued a Code of Conduct on the Safety and Security of Radioactive Sources, as discussed earlier. Its 2010-2013 Nuclear Security Plan covers the global nuclear security framework, nuclear security services, and security improvement.[27] It helps countries remove orphan radioactive sources; provides training in Asia, Africa, and South America "for regaining control over sealed sources"; and trains customs authorities in radiation monitoring.[28] It maintains an International Catalogue of Sealed Radioactive Sources and Devices to help identify sealed sources so they can be handled safely.[29]

G8 Global Partnership

In June 2002, the G8 committed to "six principles to prevent terrorists or those that harbour them from acquiring or developing" CBRN weapons, established the G8 Global Partnership Against the Spread of Weapons and Materials of Mass Destruction to implement these principles, and committed to raise "up to $20 billion" over ten years for projects supporting the partnership.[30] The partnership has many programs to reduce CBRN threats.[31]

Global Initiative to Combat Nuclear Terrorism

This initiative was established in 2006 by 13 governments.[32] Its principles include "develop, if necessary, and improve accounting, control and physical protection systems for nuclear and other radioactive materials and substances," and "improve the ability to detect nuclear and other radioactive materials and substances in order to prevent illicit trafficking in such materials and substances, to include cooperation in the research and development of national detection capabilities that would be interoperable."

U.S. Programs

National Nuclear Security Administration

Some GTRI programs seek "to identify, secure, remove and/or facilitate the disposition of high risk vulnerable nuclear and radiological materials around the world, as quickly as possible, that pose a threat to the United States and the international community."[33] The Off-site Source Recovery Project has removed 985 sources from 15 other nations as of September 2010.[34] Another NNSA program, Second Line of Defense (SLD), "strengthens the capability of foreign governments to deter, detect, and interdict illicit trafficking in nuclear and other radioactive materials across international borders and through the global maritime shipping system."[35]

Nuclear Regulatory Commission

The NRC helps regulators in other nations implement the IAEA Code of Conduct, such as by helping them develop national registries of radioactive sources, helping them with safety and security regulatory oversight, and holding workshops that describe the NRC's requirements for physical protection of materials and the U.S. regulatory framework.[36]

Department of State

The Export Control and Related Border Security (EXBS) program strengthens border security and control of strategic exports, thereby "bolster[ing] partner countries' capabilities to detect and interdict illicit transfers of strategic items, radioactive materials, and other WMD components" It assists 46 countries.[37] The Weapons of Mass Destruction

Terrorism program conducts projects to counter a terrorist CBRN attack. The department supports the Global Initiative to Combat Nuclear Terrorism.

Department of Defense

The U.S. Strategic Command coordinates global U.S. counter-CBRN efforts.[38] The Defense Threat Reduction Agency is DOD's combat support agency in this effort.[39] The two agencies operate the U.S. Strategic Command Center for Combating Weapons of Mass Destruction, which "synchronizes Combating Weapons of Mass Destruction efforts across our military's geographic commands."[40]

Programs of Other Nations

Other nations have taken steps to control their own radioactive material and to help secure such material elsewhere. Canada, in cooperation with GTRI, provided funds for removing 59 Russian radioisotopic thermoelectric generators (RTGs), which contain large amounts of radioactive material and are typically deployed unattended in remote areas.[41] Pakistan's Nuclear Regulatory Authority is implementing a National Nuclear Security Action Plan in coordination with the IAEA that manages high-risk radioactive sources, provides detection equipment at key points, and secures orphan sources.[42] Poland's state-owned Radioactive Waste Management Plant (RWMP) has been involved in the GTRI program for securing radioactive sources in Poland that has upgraded security in more than 70 institutions, including almost all oncology clinics and regional blood banks.[43] The Korean Institute for Nuclear Safety has developed a Radiation Safety Information System to trace radioactive sources through their life cycle, and a system to track misplaced or stolen industrial radiography sources in real time.[44]

How Secure Are Radioactive Sources in Other Nations?

Despite efforts to secure radioactive sources, vulnerabilities persist. The IAEA's Illicit Trafficking Database (ITDB) has data on the vulnerability of nuclear and other radioactive sources. According to the agency, "From 1 July 2009 to 30 June 2010, States reported 222 incidents to the ITDB; 120 of these were reported to have occurred during this period and the remaining 102 were reports of prior incidents. Twenty-one of the incidents reported involved such activities as unauthorized possession and/or attempts to sell or smuggle nuclear material or radioactive sources. ...One-hundred and forty reported incidents involved unauthorized activities without apparent relation to criminal activity."[45] According to the U.S. Department of State, "Of the 222 events reported to the IAEA from 1 July 2009 to 30 June 2010 involving radiological and nuclear materials outside legitimate control, most involved incidents overseas and roughly 10 percent occurred in the U.S. All of the incidents the U.S. reported to the IAEA during this time involved detections of radioactively contaminated materials coming into the U.S."[46]

In 2009, the IAEA reported "a persistent problem with illicit trafficking in nuclear and other radioactive materials, with thefts, losses and other unauthorized activities and events." Of the 1,562 confirmed incidents in the ITDB for 1995-2008, 421 involved reports of theft or loss, which IAEA called "indicative of vulnerabilities in security and control systems." Another 336 involved unauthorized possession or related criminal activities, with the number possibly higher. The 724 incidents of other unauthorized activities and events "have mainly involved radioactive sources, including some ... high-risk 'dangerous' sources, and radioactively contaminated materials. Occurrence of such incidents is an indication of failures in systems to control, secure and dispose of radioactive materials. They also show weaknesses of regulatory systems." [47]

ATTACK RESPONSE, RECOVERY, AND ATTRIBUTION

Organization and Planning for Response

If an RDD attack occurred, effective response could save lives and speed recovery. Accordingly, the federal government has planned for a response. Key authorities for response include the Stafford Act, P.L. 100-707, which authorizes the President to declare an event a disaster, thereby allowing federal agencies to assist state and local governments, the Homeland Security Act of 2002, P.L. 107-295, which establishes the Department of Homeland Security; Homeland Security Presidential Directive 5, "Management of Domestic Incidents," 2003, which makes the Secretary of Homeland Security "the principal Federal official for domestic incident management"; and the National Response Framework (NRF), which "presents the guiding principles that enable all response partners to prepare for and provide a unified national response to disasters and emergencies—from the smallest incident to the largest catastrophe."[48]

The NRF has various annexes. The Nuclear/Radiological Incident Annex "describes the policies, situations, concepts of operations, and responsibilities of the Federal departments and agencies governing the immediate response and short-term recovery activities for incidents involving release of radioactive materials."[49] It spells out which agency would have the lead or would provide support in various incidents, and the capabilities and responsibilities of each. According to the Framework, DHS would be the lead agency for "all deliberate attacks involving nuclear/radiological facilities or materials, including RDDs or INDs."[50] In 2008, FEMA issued its "Planning Guidance for Protection and Recovery Following Radiological Dispersal Device (RDD) and Improvised Nuclear Device (IND) Incidents," which provides detailed guidance on response.[51] Some states and localities have developed response plans and held exercises.

An issue for any disaster plan is how well it would work in practice. An assessment of state radiation emergency preparedness found, "in almost every measure of public health capacity and capability, the public health system remains poorly prepared to adequately respond to a major radiation emergency incident."[52] A 2011 press report raised similar concerns about national preparedness.[53] Governments have planned responses to hurricanes, yet the overall response to Hurricane Katrina was poor. The Deepwater Horizon disaster occurred despite the federal government's National Oil and Hazardous Substances Pollution Contingency Plan.

Response and Recovery

As noted earlier, FEMA divides response into early, intermediate, and late phases. The source of resources would shift with the phase. In the early phase, state and local first responders would be the primary ones available. They would focus on minimizing deaths and injuries from radiation and panic. The intermediate phase would involve higher-level care for those suffering from radiation injuries, longer-term relocation of people from areas with dangerous levels of radioactivity, and initial stages of recovery, such as decontamination. Many federal resources could be brought to bear in this phase. Late-phase efforts would focus on recovery. The main activity would be reduction of radiation hazards to an acceptable level, such as by decontaminating streets and buildings, demolishing and replacing buildings that could not be cost-effectively decontaminated, or declaring certain areas off-limits. The federal government would presumably supply the specialized expertise, techniques, equipment, and supplies required.

In 2009, President Obama directed the establishment of the White House Long-Term Disaster Recovery Working Group. It is preparing a framework document with a strategy for dealing with recovery from all disasters and a report on long-term recovery from major disasters. As of June 2011, the former is in interagency review, and the latter is in the process of gaining concurrence among the organizations drafting it. No date had been set for release of either document.[54]

Researchers have studied various decontamination methods. One study found that for radioactive materials like cesium that bond with concrete and tile, washing with water would have little effect,[55] but that a solution of water with ammonium oxalate or ammonium chloride is more effective.[56] Idaho National Laboratory is investigating the use of lasers for decontamination.[57] Argonne National Laboratory is developing a "supergel" intended "to safely capture and dispose of radioactive elements in porous structures outdoors, such as buildings and monuments, using a spray-on, super-absorbent gel and engineered nanoparticles," for use in the event of an RDD attack.[58] EPA's National Homeland Security Research Center conducts decontamination research.[59]

Attribution

If an attack occurred, the United States would surely want to retaliate against the perpetrators. Retaliation would require attribution, i.e., identifying the attacker and the source of material. Attribution relies on forensics, i.e., a fusion of evidence gathered from intelligence, law enforcement, and scientific analysis of material from the weapon. *Nuclear* forensics has been conducted for many decades. It matches samples of pre- or post-detonation weapon material to an archive of samples from facilities producing such material, or against a library of information from manufacturers. (Government agencies use "archive" to refer to a collection of physical samples and "library" to refer to a collection of information.) It looks for clues that link to other types of evidence, such as records of missing material. It identifies manufacturing processes, and may use simulation to see if a certain process could have led to a certain sample. By providing data on weapon materials and design, forensics could help determine the technical sophistication of the group that launched a nuclear attack, and which nations provided technical support, materials, or a weapon. To support this effort, the United States is developing a consolidated library and archive of nuclear material:[60] The potential to identify the source of material and the perpetrator of an attack supports deterrence and, if deterrence failed, could support retaliation.

Radiological forensics uses many of these techniques. It might be able to determine the age of a sample, perhaps eliminating some manufacturers as its source. Also, as DHS states, "non- rad[ioactive] evidence associated with the RDD will play an important role in the technical forensics investigation." Further, "Additional useful insights can be garnered from license information, sales records, vendor catalogs, etc., and this information is being collected as funding and accessibility allow."[61] The NRC and IAEA have libraries of information on sealed radioactive sources [62] that, according to one report, were not intended for forensics.[63] Since most sealed sources are made in foreign countries, DHS is funding Argonne and Idaho National Laboratories to gather data on these sources for forensics purposes.[64] Based on communications in 2011 between CRS and knowledgeable individuals at various government agencies and laboratories, there does not appear to be an archive of radioactive sources or materials.

Radiological and nuclear forensics differ in various ways. A nuclear explosion produces hundreds of radionuclides; materials that might be used in an RDD, excepting spent fuel, would likely have one or a few radionuclides, providing fewer clues. RDD radionuclides have half-lives measured in years, not hours or less, so collecting samples would not be as time-urgent as for a nuclear explosion. Nuclear forensics could support retaliation, depending on the country of origin of the material. In contrast, RDD material might be produced in one country, distributed by a second, sold to a third, and perhaps resold to a fourth, where terrorists might steal it. Argentina, Canada, several European countries, and Russia are the main producers of key radionuclides,[65] which they sell in legitimate commercial transactions, so tracing material to the producer would not provide a basis for retaliation. If terrorists obtained material through theft, illicit purchase, or an inside job, it would be hard to assign malevolent intent to the country involved.

ISSUES FOR CONGRESS

Priority for Countering Radiological Terrorism

What priority should be given to countering radiological vs. other forms of terrorism? There are many contending arguments. (1) Despite concerns about terrorist interest in RDDs, no successful RDD attack has occurred. (2) Of nuclear, chemical, biological, and radiological weapons, the latter would arguably kill the fewest people. (3) Most planning, training, equipment, and supplies that would help respond to an RDD attack would be of use in other disasters as well, so it is difficult to determine the balance between funds to counter all hazards and those to counter RDDs only. (4) Since costs resulting from an RDD attack could be tens of billions of dollars, some measures directly relevant to an RDD attack, such as decontamination R&D and securing radioactive sources, may be cost-effective.

Domestic vs. Overseas Expenditures to Secure Radioactive Sources

Where are U.S. funds to secure radioactive sources most effectively spent? One argument is that it is better to spend money to secure domestic radiological sources because if they are illicitly obtained they could be used promptly in an RDD, avoiding the risk of detection in other countries and at U.S. ports of entry. This effort would be costly. Of course, it would also be costly to secure radiological sources in countries that could not do so without international assistance. On the other hand, funds spent securing sources overseas might offer a higher benefit-cost ratio in that many sources overseas may be less secure than U.S. sources. Further, expenditures to counter the RDD threat overseas could help safeguard U.S. facilities in other nations and could help avert RDD attacks on critical facilities and infrastructure that could cause economic disruption.

Radiation Detection Networks

While attention has focused on explosive-driven "dirty bombs," an unobtrusive RDD attack could go undetected for hours, giving material time to spread and to irradiate people. A distributed network of sensors to detect, locate, and identify radioactive material would address this issue. Sensors could be mounted on buildings, police cars, or surveillance cameras. Work is underway to develop radiation-detection chips to be incorporated into cell phones or other mobile devices.[66] What would it cost to develop a detector network and deploy it in major metropolitan areas? Would it be appropriate for the federal government to fund deployment of such networks, or would deployment be a state or local responsibility?

Preparing for Decontamination

The main cost of an RDD attack would be decontamination. Proper methods depend on the RDD material, its form, types of surfaces affected, and the required decontamination level.

Decontaminators should be aware of the best techniques. Prompt availability of relevant information, such as through FEMA's Lessons Learned Information Sharing,[67] would help. Decontamination would require the proper equipment and supplies. Has the government stockpiled the needed resources or arranged to have them manufactured quickly? What areas might future R&D pursue? What is the cost of decontamination vs. demolition and reconstruction? Techniques to decontaminate areas struck by an RDD would help decontaminate the much larger area struck by radioactive fallout from an IND.

Waste Disposition and RDDs

Many studies have considered how to dispose of nuclear waste. The possibility of an RDD attack adds urgency to the disposition of radioactive waste. Most sealed sources have no disposition pathway. Choosing a permanent disposition pathway would reduce the risk of terrorists obtaining this material. On a larger scale, decontamination would generate chemicals, water, and radioactive material. How would this waste be handled? If decontamination proved ineffective, an alternative would be to demolish contaminated buildings, generating much rubble. Where would it go? If buried, would it contaminate the water table? If it were to be buried out of state, would another state accept it? How would it be transported? Would states along the proposed route try to block transit? It would appear more efficient to plan in advance how to dispose of this rubble rather than deciding on a rushed basis postattack.

Materials Protection

The GTRI Domestic Materials Protection Program visits facilities requesting its service, examines the security situation, and installs security devices. It provides this service on a voluntary basis at no initial cost to the facilities. As of February 2011, it had "identified more than 2,700 vulnerable buildings ... with high-priority radioactive material in the United States," had completed security enhancements at 251 of the buildings, "with the remainder aiming to be completed by 2025."[68] Other upgrades will take several years as well. Alternatives include expanding this program to complete upgrades sooner, maintaining it at its current level, eliminating it, or making it mandatory.

Radiological Forensics

Congress has given nuclear forensics strong support, so it may wish to strengthen radiological forensics capability. Since radiological forensics is typically grouped with nuclear forensics, Congress could establish a panel to examine the unique aspects and requirements of the former and how its science and technology might be advanced. Congress could also support the buildout of archives of samples relevant to RDDs.

End Notes

[1] The most common types of particles emitted in decay are alpha particles (two protons plus two neutrons), beta particles (an electron or positron, with the latter being a positively-charged electron), and, for heavy elements, neutrons.

[2] National Council on Radiation Protection and Measurement, *Ionizing Radiation Exposure of the Population of the United States,* report 160 (2009), available via http://www.ncrppublications.org/Reports/160. The figure of 620 mrem is from "NCRP Report No. 160 Section 1 Pie Chart," http://www.ncrponline.org/ Publications/160_Pie_charts-Sec1.html.

[3] 10 CFR 190.10(a).

[4] 20 CFR 1201(a)(1)(i).

[5] U.S. Environmental Protection Agency. Office of Radiation Programs. *Manual of Protective Action Guides and Protective Actions for Nuclear Incidents,* revised 1991; and Federal Emergency Management Agency, "Planning Guidance for Protection and Recovery

Following Radiological Dispersal Device (RDD) and Improvised Nuclear Device (IND) Incidents," 73 *Federal Register* 45029-45048, August 1, 2008.

[6] Ibid., p. 45034.

[7] Quotes in this paragraph are from ibid., pp. 45032 and 45035.

[8] International Atomic Energy Agency, *Code of Conduct on the Safety and Security of Radioactive Sources,* January 2004, http://www.iaea.org/Publications/Booklets/ RadioactiveSources/radioactivesource.pdf.

[9] Ibid., p. 2.

[10] Ibid., p. 15.

[11] National Research Council. *Radiation Source Use and Replacement, Abbreviated Version*, p. 7.

[12] Nuclear Regulatory Commission, "Physical Protection of Byproduct Material: Proposed Rule," 75 *Federal Register* 33902, June 15, 2010.

[13] JiYoung Park, "The Economic Impacts of Dirty Bomb Attacks on the Los Angeles and Long Beach Ports: Applying the Supply-Driven NIEMO (National Interstate Economic Model," *Journal of Homeland Security and Emergency Management,* vol. 5, no. 1 (2008), article 21, p. 10, http://www.bepress.com/jhsem/vol5/iss1/21/.

[14] See Nuclear Threat Initiative, *Radiological Terrorism Tutorial,* "History of Radiological Incidents."

[15] U.S. Nuclear Regulatory Commission. "Request for Comments on the Draft Policy Statement on the Protection of Cesium-137 Chloride Sources and Notice of Public Meeting," NRC-2010-0209, *Federal Register,* vol. 75, no. 124, June 29, 2010, p. 37484.

[16] Los Alamos National Laboratory, "OSRP Sources Recovered," as of March 28, 2011, http://osrp.lanl.gov/images/ Maps/Recoveries_to_Date.pdf.

[17] U.S. Radiation Source Protection and Security Task Force. *The 2010 Radiation Source Protection and Security Task Force Report,* August 2010, http://www.nrc.gov/security

[18] U.S. Environmental Protection Agency. "Alternative Technologies for Industrial Applications," http://www.epa.gov/radiation/source-reduction-management/alt-technologies.html.

[19] Information provided by Chemical, Biological, Radiological, and Nuclear Directorate, Office of Homeland Defense Integration and Defense Support of Civil Authorities, Office of the Secretary of Defense, Department of Defense, personal communication, September 15, 2010, and by Nuclear Regulatory Commission, February 10, 2011.

[20] U.S. Nuclear Regulatory Commission. "Security Inspections and Enforcement," briefing slides 5-8, no date. NRC provided these slides to CRS July 31, 2010.

[21] U.S. Radiation Source Protection and Security Task Force. *The 2010 ... Report,* p. 31.

[22] Personal communication, Nuclear Regulatory Commission, November 30, 2010.

[23] U.S. Nuclear Regulatory Commission. "Security Inspections and Enforcement," slide 19.

[24] Idaho National Laboratory, "Nuclear Material Events Database: Quarterly Report, Second Quarter Fiscal Year 2010," by Thomas Smith and Robert Sant, INL/EXT-10-18136 (FY 2010 Qtr 2), July 2010, p, 5.

[25] National Commission on Terrorist Attacks upon the United States, *The 9/11 Commission Report,* New York, Norton, 2004, p. vii.

[26] "A Ticking Time Bomb: Counterterrorism Lessons from the U.S. Government's Failure to Prevent the Fort Hood Attack," a special report by Joseph I. Lieberman, Chairman, and Susan M. Collins, Ranking Member, United States Senate Committee on Homeland Security and Governmental Affairs, February 3, 2011, p. 53.

[27] International Atomic Energy Agency. Board of Governors. General Conference. "Nuclear Security Plan 2010-2013." GOV/2009/54-GC(53)/18, August 17, 2009, pp. 8-12.

[28] International Atomic Energy Agency, "Improving the Safety and Security of Sealed Radioactive Sources," accessed May 2, 2011, http://www.iaea.org/Publications/Booklets/ SealedRadioactiveSources/activities.html.

[29] International Atomic Energy Agency, "International Catalogue of Sealed Radioactive Sources and Devices (ICSRS)," http://nucleusupdated 2010.

[30] G8, "The G8 Global Partnership Against the Spread of Weapons and Materials of Mass Destruction," June 27, 2002.

[31] G8, "Report on the G-8 Global Partnership 2010," last modified February 11, 2011.

[32] For links to key documents on the Global Initiative, see U.S. Department of State. "The Global Initiative To Combat Nuclear Terrorism," http://www.state

[33] U.S. Department of Energy. National Nuclear Security Administration. "GTRI: Reducing Nuclear Threats," January 2009, http://www.nnsa.energy

[34] Los Alamos National Laboratory, Off-site Source Recovery Program, "OSRP Operations Worldwide."

[35] Department of Energy, *FY 2011 Congressional Budget Request.* volume 1, p. 371.

[36] U.S. Nuclear Regulatory Commission and National Nuclear Security Administration, *Partnership for Securing Nuclear and Radiological Materials*, March 31, 2010, p. 2.

[37] U.S. Department of State., *Fiscal Year 2011 Congressional Budget Justification: Volume 2, Foreign Operations*, 2010, p. 176, http://www.state.gov/documents/organization/137936.pdf.

[38] U.S. Strategic Command. "USSTRATCOM Center for Combating Weapons of Mass Destruction (SCC-WMD)," February 2011.

[39] U.S. Department of Defense. Defense Threat Reduction Agency and USSTRATCOM Center for Combating WMD. "About DTRA/SCC-WMD," http://www.dtra.mil/About.aspx.

[40] Ibid.

[41] Canada. Department of Foreign Affairs and International Trade. Personal communication, May 24, 2011.

[42] Embassy of Pakistan, Washington, DC, personal communication, May 17, 2011.

[43] Information provided to CRS by the National Atomic Energy Agency, Warsaw, Poland, May 16, 2011.

[44] Republic of Korea, Korea Institute of Nuclear Safety, "Country Report on (RAS/9/042), 'Sustainability of Regional Radiation Protection Infrastructure,'" 2009, p. 22.

[45] International Atomic Energy Agency, Board of Governors, *Nuclear Security Report 2010: Measures to Protect Against Nuclear Terrorism*, Report by the Director General, GOV/2010/42-GC(54)/9, August 12, 2010, p. 4.

[46] Personal communication, Department of State, May 6, 2011.

[47] Material on ITDB in this paragraph is from International Atomic Energy Agency, "IAEA Illicit Trafficking Database (ITDB)," September 2009, pp. 1-5, http://wwwns.iaea.org/downloads/security/itdb-fact-sheet-2009.pdf.

[48] For further information on the National Response Framework, see U.S. Department of Homeland Security. Federal Emergency Management Agency. "NRF Resource Center," http://www.fema.gov/emergency

[49] U.S. Department of Homeland Security. Federal Emergency Management Agency. "Nuclear/Radiological Incident Annex," June 2008, p. NUC-1, http://www.fema.gov/pdf/emergency/nrf/nrf_nuclearradiologicalincidentannex.pdf.

[50] Ibid., p. NUC-9.

[51] U.S. Department of Homeland Security. Federal Emergency Management Agency. "Planning Guidance for Protection and Recovery Following Radiological Dispersal Device (RDD) and Improvised Nuclear Device (IND) Incidents," notice of final guidance, *Federal Register,* vol. 73, no. 149, August 1, 2008. pp. 45029-45048.

[52] Council of State and Territorial Epidemiologists, "The Status of State-Level Radiation Emergency Preparedness and Response Capabilities, 2010," October 6, 2010, p. 13, http://www.cste.org/webpdfs/2010raditionreport.pdf.

[53] Sheri Fink, "U.S. Health-Care Systems Said to Be Unprepared for Nuclear Disaster" *Washington Post,* March 8, 2011, p. 3.

[54] Personal communication, Federal Emergency Management Agency, June 14, 2011.

[55] J. Real et al., "Mechanisms of Desorption of 134Cs [cesium-134] and 85Sr [strontium-85] Aerosols Deposited on Urban Surfaces," *Journal of Environmental Radioactivity*, 62 (2002), p. 1.

[56] Ibid., p. 1.

[57] Mike Wall, "INL Laser Research Could Help U.S. Respond to Terror Attack," April 19, 2010.

[58] Argonne National Laboratory. "'Supergel' System for Cleaning Radioactively Contaminated Structures."

[59] U.S. Environmental Protection Agency. Homeland Security Research. http://www.epa.gov/nhsrc/. The center's reports on RDDs are available at http://tinyurl.com/3kfyntf.

[60] "Statement of Rolf Mowatt-Larssen, Director of the Office of Intelligence and Counterintelligence, United States Department of Energy, before the Homeland Security and Governmental Affairs Committee, United States Senate, April 2, 2008," in U.S. Congress. Senate. Committee on Homeland Security and Governmental Affairs. Hearings. "Nuclear Terrorism: Assessing the Threat to the Homeland," April 2, 2008.

[61] Information provided by Department of Homeland Security, email, May 17, 2010.

[62] See International Atomic Energy Agency, "International Catalogue of Sealed Radioactive Sources and Devices (ICSRS)"; and U.S. Nuclear Regulatory Commission. "Sealed Source and Device Registry: Supplement for 10 CFR Part 35 Uses."

[63] Margaret Goldberg and Martha Finck, "International Data on Radiological Sources," Idaho National Laboratory, INL/CON-10-18939, Preprint, July 2010, p. 3, http://www.inl.gov/technicalpublications/Documents/4633185.pdf.

[64] Ibid.

[65] National Research Council. *Radiation Source Use and Replacement, Abbreviated Version*, p. 41.

[66] Benjamin Sutherland, "My Blackberry as a Bomb Sniffer?," *Newsweek*, September 27, 2008; Emil Venere and Elizabeth Gardner, "Cell Phone Sensors Detect Radiation to Thwart Nuclear Terrorism," Purdue University news release, January 22, 2008; and personal communication, Simon Labov, Associate Program Leader for Detection Systems, Lawrence Livermore National Laboratory, February 14, 2011.

[67] U.S. Department of Homeland Security. Federal Emergency Management Agency. "Lessons Learned Information Sharing," https://www.llis.dhs.gov/index.do.

[68] U.S. Department of Energy. National Nuclear Security Administration. "NNSA: Securing Domestic Radioactive Material," fact sheet, February 1, 2011, p. 2.

INDEX